The Heritage Monuments of Matsyadesa of Mahabharat

The one year 'agayantabasa' (disguised living)as per the rule after defeat in pasha"(royal gambling)the Paandava's came far away of Hastinapur(Delhi)to Matsyadesa"where these relics are found.

ISBN 978-93-5667-810-1
© Janaki Ballav Dash 2023

Published in India 2023 by Pencil

Contributors:
Co-Author: Nainika Dash
Co-Author: Nainika Dash

A brand of
One Point Six Technologies Pvt. Ltd.
Unit no. 26, Ground Floor, Building A1,
Wadala Truck Terminal Road,
Near Post Office, Antop Hill, Mumbai - 400037
E connect@thepencilapp.com
W www.thepencilapp.com

Author biography

JANAKI BALLAV DASH,a scholar,national fellow

CONTENTS

The Heritage Monuments of Matsyadesa of Mahabharat

HERITAGE MONUMENTS OF MATSYADESA-MAYURBHANJ AND BHANJA RULERS
Heritage Buildings, Structures, Monuments, sites of Mahabharat Era and Bhanja Rulers
JANAKI BALLAV DASH

CHAPTERS : SECTION -A
The Journey for Mahabharatian era sites:
Raibania Fort
Prehistoric Mahabharatian era site
Prehistoric site in Mayurbhanj
Itagarh, Dubigarh-Mahabharatian era site
Mahabharatian era site-Samibrukhya
KuliamalamMeru Math, Basudev Temple
Kainsari Fort
Mahabharatian heritage-Maa Kichakeswari
Mahabharatian interaction
Paanchpidh-Abode of Paandava's
Reign of Five-Panchpidh
Keshna-derivatives of Krishna
BenuMadhav Matha-Paandava's worship place
Khiching-cultural-geographic boundaries
Benisagar-The mythical Place of Paanchali

Kakharua Baidyanath
Manatri & Kuradiha garh
Baruneswar Mahadev
Sanskriti Bhavan
Simleshwar pitha
Purnachandra Mandir
Baripada club
Banthia Jaganath Mandir
Christian cemetery
Maa Hingula pitha
NH Inspection bunglow
Circuit House
Railaways-Narrow & Broad gauge
Baptist Church
Maa Santoshi Temple
Bamanghati Garhi temple
Ma Kichakeswarigarh-Bahalda
Dandbose Air strip
MaharajaKrushnachandra Highschool
SuryaNivas
Highcourt-Mayurbhanj
Durbar Admn-Mayurbhanj state Bank
Localself Govt-Baripada Municipality
Maa Jwalamukhi Temple
Karamparva-cultural fiesta
Kurmis cultural demand
Deokund-A major shaktipitha
Kamardiha Matha-A ruinous site
Cremation place or personal holdings
Sarada Mandir
Saraskshetra of Lord Jaganath
Chahla Heritage resthouse

Nagrabhadi heritage building
Maa Kichakeswari Baripada Temple
Maingate of Belgadia palace
Sri Haribaladevjew temple
Heritage Mayurbhanj Palace
Mayurbhanj State Bank
Resthouse Nichuapada
Heritage Maharani Dharmasala
Maa Dwarsuni Mandir
Jhinkeswar Mahadev
Dalimbeswar Mahadev, Kainsari
Baptist church
Heritage Christian cemetery
Heritage Jubilee library
Kichakeswari-Bahalda
ASIs neglect-Itagarh, Dubigarh
Kakharua Baidyanath pitha
Deokund
Maharaja Sri Ramchandra Bhanj statue
Maa Hingula pitha
Seva sangha heritage building

Acknowledgement

The Fellow Author expresses his sincere gratitude with Thanks to all in the Ministry of Culture, Govt. of India for its kind & unconditional Support for this documentation work, without which it couldn't have been possible.

This documentation is dedicated with a hope that the future generation would come to terms with our aeon-old tradition, culture and the govt would make all these virgin spot-sites believed to be of Mahabharata era during Paandava's agayatabasa of a year to develop these as major, important heritage tourist sites on the roadmap provided here. It is an humble attempt to unearth the Matsyadesa in today's Mayurbhanj & all those aspects which signify these beliefs.

Senior Fellow

PREFACE

It is a lifetime opportunity to be a part of history-maker in contributing to strengthen those myths, pables which are in circulation since long, although in a distorted manner. Since my childhood, there were inebriated attempt by few to amplify the beliefs that – Mayurbhanj was the Matsyadesa of Mahabharata – and from this one sentence, starts the development of this intensive research study. The many myths, relics, heritage sites and special characteristics lend belief to this thought which has resulted in this monumental work, a maiden attempt to amplify those aspects, sites which form a distinct part of Paandava's sojourn.

Mahabharat-the great epic of yore describes the 'agayatabasa'(living in hiding)of Pandava's for one year when they came from far off Hastinapur (modern Delhi) to 'Birat Raja's state,then known as 'Matsyadesa'.Today's Mayurbhanj district & earlier Mayurbhanj Gadjat state'is known to be "Matsyadesa'of Mahabharata, as the remains of fort of Birat Raja and Kichak temple and the place in which the five Pandava's have hid their weapons, bears testimony to this place. This region left many monuments, sites to those rulers of Mahabharat era and thereafter Mughal, Maratha, British & Bhanja Kings who have mightily contributed to this region in the form of many buildings, structures, monuments, heritage sites etc.which are presently on ths ruins, due to apathetism & lack of important data, documentation on each of these sites, whose proper documentation can pave the way for its conservation & protection for humanity. The area has remained under the rule of popular Bhanja Kings for a considerable period of time who hails from Rajputana i.e. Jaipur in modern Rajasthan in 598 A.D and the first King was Maharaja Jai Singh and since than the 'Bhanja dynasty' has ruled this region with 56 successive rulers till its merger in 1949 with Indian Union and became a part of Odisha, adjacent to Bihar, Bengal & Jharkhand. The benevolent Bhanja rulers ushered the golden age during their period which was manifested in different art & architecture,monuments & buildings,temples & palaces ;a number of which have already been ruined, extincted and many such heritage sites & buildings are on the verge of fast extinction, due to the onslaught of modern construction process and growing human habitation.

Since this study also equally laid stress on the documentation of actual sites it covers a whole gamut of areas, regions personally covered by the fellow in an intensive field study vigorously to capture those remains of Mahabharatian era. These photographic details provide more flesh to the bone- of -belief that it was the Matsyadesa and once upon a time Pandava's presence in this soil had blistered it with magnanimous power.

Due efforts have been taken to incorporate all such actual sites but inadvertent omissions if any be rectified by the Fellow-author in upcoming versions.All such sites,places,structures,monuments have been covered under 'Bhanja Vignette'.

Senior Fellow

SECTION : A

Raibania Fort

The Journey for Mahabharat era sites: An exploration which establishes a point that – Raja Biraat fort –where weapons like Arjuna's Gandiva and kichaka fort or The Pandava's undertook journey from far –off Hastinapur (present Delhi) to Matsyadesa during their sojourn of one year agayatabasa, like wise this journey of Mahabharatian site has been started from Raibania, the legendary site & remains of Raja Biraat of Mahabharat fame situated at about 36 km from Balasore, 66 km from Mayurbhanj. The area passes through famous & the only air strip of eastern India.The road from Denganalia village to the Biraat Raja's fort site of about 16 km are muddy, inaccessible & presently the Pradhanmantri gramsadak yojana is being carried out for which it is almost impossible to pass on the under-constructed road. However with much difficulty after reaching the spot,popularly known as Raibania fort here whose distance of 3 km from main road to the fort was under construction with Rs 16 lakh assistance from local MP Kharavela Swain who took the initiative during last two years to construct a pucca road known here as Gadachandi road to the fort site of this Mahabharat era.The area is surrounded by many smaller & big ponds, tanks which according to the villagers have been named such as – Kaushalya, Jaljantra, Kundigadia, Bhuynapokhari, Nandiaka, Digi.The fort bears the testimony of Biraat Raja of Mahabharat fame where the Paanch-Paandavas came to complete their 'agayatabasa'.His brother in law Raja Kichaka of Mahabharat fame had his own fort around 250 km from this place which defines this region as 'Matsyadesa'during Mahabharat era.There is a popular saying in odiya here 'kichaka bahubale Birat raja' means Biraat is king under the powerful arm, strength of his brother-in-law Kichaka.The fort is completely ruined except around 10/15 feets of boundary walls and a gate.The inside of the fort has become heaps of stones & debris depicting the unique style of those era.A spot where local people called it to be the bathing place of Maharani's have underground stairs which if undertaken can open many new insights. It is known from local gentry sources that the excavation by some officials some years back were too short & stopped due to want of funds & since than it is remaining in this stage, as several photographs depicts this. The fort is surrounded with a Devi Kichaki, the popular deity who guards the fort & anyone trying to photograph HER simply yields black on print. With local community involvement a Shiva temple is under completion.The deity has a unique major festival during Panasankranti of april 14 every year.The fort was last stated to be in possession of Rai Bahadur Singh, a zamindar of the area and thereafter it become a govt.property,but no steps were taken to declare it as a major historic heritage site, property or never undertaken by ASI or any other conservation departments for which it is further on the ruins.The local people now guards this Mahabharat era fort zone zealously and narrates many anecdotes of those days which has been enliven on hearsay like how the Pandavas took shelter at Biraat Raja, Draupadi was hiding with his queen & how Kichaka saw her feet etc to the days relates to Mahabharat era and thereafter by Maharatta's attack on this area, fort ;Kalapahad's attack on this fort & laments the vivid historicity of those days today known as Khiching on which the exploration progresses. However after the embarking of several visits by this author to the Raibania area it is found that, a group of local youths have formed a Raibania Suraksha Samity to safeguard the deteriorating fort with kolkatta's ASI being step into takeup protection,excavation work soon.

Prehistoric-Mahabharatian era site

The prehistoric Mahabharatian era site is situated in the foothills of famous Similipal sanctuary in Kaptipada subdivision-block of Podadiha Panchayat and the area is known as- Itagarh & Sanjunpal.Way back to 1995 the Archaeological Survey of India(ASI) team had undertook an excavation and curved out a number of things like iron ammunitions, iron quiver, soil-stone-iron-pots, utensils, burnt bricks etc. It was known from the locality that two former ASI officials Debendra Barik, Prasanta Ray in coordination with a retired teacher & a social orgn.- Sankarsan Pradhan & Jatiya Seba Pratisthana respectively had initiated its preliminary survey, findings. And it was during those years the author being a part of the social orgn.then had an opportunity to study it which resulted into very unique findings. It was also a popular belief among the locals here that the entire Similipal area needs to be exclusively reserve as a protected site so as to preserve many relics, things, materials of Mahabharatian era as Raja Biraat & his brother in law Kichaka's domain was found in this region and part of this area comes under it – stated many historians, researchers while depicting the Mahabharat fame 'Matsyadesa', popularly known today as Mayurbhanj. A number of representative findings, claims published documented earlier in the local language by this author have given momentum to this further exploration & study.

Prehistoric Mahabharatian era site:Sathilo

Another prehistoric Mahabharatian site Sathilo is a grampanchayat under Betnoti block in Mayurbhanj.The village is found with very ancient sites of ruin of a fort.These ruinous fort has been covered with two ponds from each of its sides.It was stated by village elders that there was a fort along with a temple worshipped by some rulers belongs to Bhanja kings although many contest this view. However few years ago the local population on their own initiatives have digged the area and found some stone slabs having artistic figures, curvings, images of deities like Durga, Nursingha, SriKrishna and kept those in a local temple.Today the ruinous of the said area has completely razed to the ground and the entire heritage area has been densely populated with number of houses.The particular site of the ruinous fort has been now under the occupation of one Nilakantha Mohapatra who said he has purchased this piece of land from one Bengali, Mani Babu long ago on inquiry by the author.However here is no remnants of fort except some land level bricks and the entire heritage zone was never excavated by Archaeological Survey of India (ASI) and thus a gorgeous heritage site on the route to Kolkata-Chennai highway has gone into memory of public minds in this locality.

Probable Pre-historic Mahabharatian sites

Mayurbhanj state otherwise famous as Matsyadesa of Mahabharat period houses many historic,heritage sites and after much research a view on this subject ,numbers of such sites were enlisted.Many such historic-heritage sites dating back to stone age,prehistoric age,monolithic period donot have any remains although some have few important relics & remains to boost such claims viz;

Khiching, Pratappur, Muruda, Kaptipada, Baidipur, Bahlda, Kuchei, Mahulia, Deosole, Bisoi, Dahikothi sasan, Ambdali sasan, Mananda, Amsikd, Jadipal to name a few.Such places have been glorify by their ancientness & possession of many heritageness like unique culture,art,crafts,designwares etc.The study has charted out all such heritage sites after taking primay observation from different quarters .

Itagarh, Dubigarh-Mahabharatian era sites

The famous Mahabharatian era sites where remains,cultural folklore especially of the agayatabasa(hideout)of Paandavas is famous in this region.Interestingly the author since long have come across through many such materials from the few short stories & folklores from the elders.But during the course of this study it has been crystal clear that Paandava's during their agayatabasa of one year came from Hastinapur,Kurukshetra(modern Delhi region) to hide themselves in such a way that for one full year,the Kaurava's could not recognize them and incase they have been recognized or identified by them during this period,they would again have to go to vanavasa for another twelve years. Such crucial condition in their victory might have forced the Pandava's to far off places like Matsyadesa or popularly known today as Mayurbhanj.Accordingly Paandvas redesignted themselves as follows to reach this place which was ruled by then valiant ruler Kichaka and his brother in law Raja Biraat.Yudhistira named himself as Kanka-a Brahmin;Bhima known as Ballabha,the cook;Arjuna as Bruhannalla-the music teacher;Nakula the Ashwapalak as horse care taker,Sahadev as Gopala,the caretaker of cows in the palace of king Biraat and Draupadi as Sudeshna/Sairindhri,the courtesan to Maharani of Biraat Raja.It is a rare opportunity to visit this palace site of Biraat Raja which is popularly known here as Dubigarh(immersed fort) & Itagarh(fort of bricks). This place is just exists in the foothills of famous Similipal sanctuary & biosphere reserve. Dubigarh is inside the curvical mountaneous range of Similipal. The locals stated that there is a walkable route to Dubigarh but it is very tedious, dangerous as it is in the hilltop. They further said that Dubigarh was once the palace of Raja Biraat who gave shelter to the Paandavs during their agayatabasa of a year. There was a huge place which lateron with the passage of time have been covered under stone heaps, thick bushes & jungles of different kinds.In the opposite sides of Biraat's palace two ponds popularly known as Raja & Rani pokhari is found even today which were perhaps used by kings & queens respectively.Despite the best of efforts it could not possible to reach the exact location of Dubigarh inview of big stone slabs & attempting to reach the exact spot to capture the Biraat-gada (fort). However a number of photographs of this place from a distance were captured which gives a shape to the existing footway to the palace area. Just below it, on the ground level is situated Itagarh where a small village & an ashram school exists. Just adjacent to the ashram school there are cultivable lands and the village elders took the fellow-author amidst their land to the exact point where 15 years ago the ASI undertook an excavation but since then left this work midway which has gradually covered up with muds,bushes,grass fields. In this excavation of ASI there was some remains found dating back to Mahabharatian era according to many historian.The area is famous as Itagarh where bricks of unusual size was used as in Haripur fort.The elders said that, the entire area if excavated would give new meanings to Mahabharatian era proofs which was abandoned due to huge expenses.The area has been documented with several photographs.

Mahabharatian era site: Sami-brukhya

Perhaps this particular site speaks the story of Paandava's agayatabasa stay, as many remains, cultural folklores of their weapons hiding in this particular place known as Sami-brukhya exhibits. It is situated around 12 km from the fort of Biraat Raja near Dubigarh.Infact Itagarh, Dubigarh forts which are situated in the foothills of famous Similipal sanctuary is the region where Samibrukhya falls. Situated on the river bed of Kushabhadra in Radho village of Podadiha under Udala subdivision, this spot exudes a mystery of heritageness along with a sense of presence of mighty Paandava's. When one reaches the village Kulialam a narrow road greets the visitors to take into this mysterious zone upto river Kushabhadra where a matha' situated.There is no permanent bridge over this river and during Makar-sankranthi a big mela of local community is organized on the past glory of pandava's which lasts upto a fortnight.The pathways from the riverbed to Samibrukhya is tedious,rocky and muddy which is around one km.and this Mahabharatian era heritage site has filled one with a sense of awe,air of mystery & spine chilling visuals,as if the paandva's are greeting with their holy presence.

Samibrukhya,the odiya translation of a particular tree where the Paandava's reportedly hid their weapons & armoury during agayatabasa, on the core of this big tree,is no more a tree today.As elders since generations have gathered many anecdotes pass on to their future generation about the pandavas arms hiding tree which has turned today into a big rocky mountain with thousands of trees sprouted from this holy mountaneous range.Visitors,tourists have been able to ride on upto an extent of this tree-turned-mountain which is very difficult to climb.There are many folklores among the locality that,the particular spot of the tree-core where pandavas hided their arms were always guarded by poisonous big snakes of mammoth size as described in scriptures but never seen to bare eyes of human beings. During field visits to this area it has been covered with number of photo-documntation featue and found that many small caves have developed encompassing this tree-mountain range and possibly such hideous places inside in this hilly forest range be used by paandava's during Mahabharat era.

Kulialam Matha & Basudev Temple

The presence of Kulialam-math where Basudev Temple (Shri Krishna) just beneath this Samibrukhya, a range further connotes & establish the presence of Shri Krishna & Panchu-Paandava's. As usually this area has been infested with many deities, mostly Goddess, but here in this particular spot it is amazing to find a Shri Krishna-Basudev place of worship.This matha is also famous as polar worship place of pandava's. Elders,researchers and stories lend support to the view that,the paandava's came from Hastinapur on agayatabasa from one corner to another,i.e,from one polarity to another and perhaps they might have renamed this place which was ideal for their hiding,even today also and as they were great worshippers of Lord Shri Krishna,they had built this Basudev temple in this polarity, known as kulialam matha.The place is very calm,serene and one would instantly feel the presence of paandava's and their mentor Sri Krishna, as if one is getting drown into the Mahabharat-past zone.This matha is guarded by a sadhu known as Jaganath Das who worship the Basudeva everyday.The demand for better management of this Mahabharatian era matha has been vested with a trust board and the subcollector,Udala is its executive officer which looks after its management.But seeing things as they are ,one would easily find a conclusion that,the officials didn't gave the shrine the needed care nor funds for which it looks dilapidated.The matha has few acres of landed property and its harvest annually is the only continuous source of income for the nitipuja of deity.The only other occasion it receives dakshina is when Makarsankranthi sets in. A former local MP has given 2.50 lakh for construction of a storehouse which is used as police outpost during the mela and round the year it houses the paddy,rice of the matha poperty.The photographing details of this place filled one with a sense of connectedness to the pristine past,heritageous glory of this Mahabharatian era site.A report published by this author has given the locals perception that this heritage site is gradually sinking down the Kushabhadra river and the matter was takenup for road-bridge in this area and NABARD has agreed to pledge around 1.60 Crore for construction of bridge on river Kushabhadra,thus directly connecting to this Mahabharat era heritage relics.

Mahabharatian heritage: Kainsari Fort

A visit to Kainsari rea where once a fort was built of the Mahabharatian era bears a mystical testimonyeven to this day .The Bhanja rulers have constructed a number of forts in the glory of their scions and to uphold royalty and one such remnants is Kainsari Fort. The fort was dating back to Raja -Biraat of Mahabharat fame. Many elders believe and it has pass on to generation that, it was the Capital of Raja Biraat of Mahabharat fame. The areas situated in present Udala subdivisions. Many also believes that this area was once the penance-ashram of famous sage of Mahabharat, Uddalaka, from which the present day name of Udala derived. The Fellow during the interaction with local elders at Kainsari chronicled that – this was the place of famous Mahabharatian sage Uddalaka as well as the Capital of Raja Biraat. This fort was enjoyed by second line royalty of Bhanja kings having the title of 'sai' or 'das' who usually accompany the surname Biraat Raja, for instance onc of the name of princely rulers was – Nanu Sai Biraat Raja, Shatrughan Das Biraat Raja. It gives one a very amazing feelings that the rulers of this fort was adding a suffix 'Biraat Raja' with their names which was nowhere found in this region or any other region of India. This signifies that they were the descendants of Raja Biraat, who were adding the suffix of Raja Viraat with their names.

The fort site was located amidst a narrow village road and at the end of village jungle one finds the remnants of a fort. The entire fort area has been covered under heaps of clay and a hilly-top look is found except the edges of old boundary wall. Here is a 'gada-chandi devi' as was worshipped in all the forts of Mahabharatian era which is also worshipped now. The entire fort area was donated some years back by the descendants of Nanusai Viraat Raja family to govt. which has constructed & running the Kainsari primary school. Instead of fighting for the fort-land, we donate it for greater public cause to that of imparting primary education to the less privileged children in this area, said Shatrughan Das Babu Viraat Raja, who prefers to drop the suffix of Viraat Raja from his name and simply like to call him in his name. This means gradually the descendants of Raja Viraat feels to drop this surname in this stiff competitive world where Values and cultures are no longer worshipped unless humanity faces major hurdles. The descendants are poor but having the dignity of their great predecessor Raja Viraat and still manages the Dalimbeswar Mahadev temple built by some of their ancestors. The photo documentation a number of historic yet ravaged area from this Kainsari fort site which reminds one the glorious past of yester years, on this Bhanja lands. The presence of Mahabharatian era culture has another substance one can find in the recently made demands of several political parties of this region. Mayurbhanj-the state was merged in 1949 with Indian Union and after 60 years of its annexation, it is deprived and undeveloped in every sector; blame it to its poor leadership or stepmotherly treatment that demands for its further division in separate districts and later on for curvingout the Viraat-state was a interesting phenomena. Because such political demands have different undertones but in this region, there is a demand for Viraat-state, which indicates that there is presence of Mahabharatian era heritages, cultures, and Viraat Raja, a tangible testimony to the subtle evidences.

Mahabhartian era site: Dhudeswarpitha-Baruni- Khunta

Another important Mahabharatian era relics is the place popularly known as Dhudeswar-pitha or Dhudeswar baruni.It is nearby to Khunta block bazaar in Mayurbhanj district or the pristine Matsyadesa of Mahabharat fame.The area comprises of Ghantasila mountain range wherein legends & relics shows that several mountaineous rocks having imprints of the knee mark of mighty Bhima. This mountain also have a number of relics of Arjuna's footprints searching for arrows according to many elders. The area is said to be habitated by mighty Paandava's during their one year agayatabasa in this Matsyadesa. Dhudeswar is the name of Lord Shiva here which houses this Mahabharatian era relics in its stones, jungles & rocky mountains and stories of culturally inherited generationswise about many myths of Paandava's sojourn in this Matsyadesa region. Situated in the bordering villages of Sankhunta, Titia, Bhandgaon comprises this famous Pannadava's legendary place nearby which river Gangahaar is flowing.The Shiva, believed to be appeared on this rocky river bed of Gangahaar which hides it round the year inside the rocks except during Baruni-snan',makar sankranti and to have a darshan'on this auspicious day believing they would attain moksha' on this day. Apart from Dhudeswar barunipitha this Mahabharatian era relics also houses some other important tourists places such as Delingi -bandha, Mahimadharma Sunya mandir on Tangrahudi(name of a mountain),centennial Nrusingha Baba Mahima ashram near Naluha river on this scenic spot which immediately transport a visitor to the era of Mahabharat with the several myths of mighty Paandava's.This site has remained under complete oblivion from visitors eye so far as illegal mining activities have already damaged major portion of this historic mountaneous range believed to be blessed with the marks of mighty Paandava's -Bhima & Arjuna's physical strength as well as serenity.

Mahabharatian interaction

The attempt to bring back the ancient memory of this Matsyadesa of Mahabharat fame, presently named as Mayurbhanj, the Fellow had interacted with two scholars in this regard and brought the ambience of Mahabharat fame matsyadesa which is symmetrically manifesting on observance of folklore, physical structures along with repleting memory of localities. The biggest discovery is: there is an area known as Paanch-pidh which is locally known as 'village for five' which have villages/areas in the names of Paanch-pandavas of Mahabharat fame. These are Arjuna-pidh or village-Arjuna Judhistir-pidh, Bhim-pidh etc which many believes that, perhaps habitated by the Paandavs during their agyaat -basa to this region, far away from Hastinapur. However no scholars or researchers of repute have worked upon this idea so far which is gaining strengthen with evidences of Paandavas- agyaatbasa period in this matsyadesa - Mayurbhanj.

Paanchpidh – Abode of Paandavas

The several field visits undertook for research-visits to a number of places, replete with Mahabharatian era glories & having tangible existence of evidences largely associated with Paandavas. In this Matsyadesa of Mahabharat era fame today known as Mayurbhanj, Here is a region popularly known as Paanch-pidh i.e, places of five which gives historical justification as well as evidences of Mahabharatian era, more specifically the period of agyaatbasa of panchu-paandavas. As stated earlier the Paandavas along with Draupadi came to this region, then the Raja Biraat's kingdom & Kichaka's palaces and hid their weapons in a mountain named Samibrukhya. The region where Paandavas were staying, came to be famous & known as paanch-pidh,the place of five which today also bears this name and panchpidh is a subdivision under this present Mayurbhanj district .The most famous heritage site in this region is Kichaka's fort,the deity called Kichakeswari .This area is popularly known as Khiching today which earlier knew as Khijingkota .The Bhanja rulers have had their kingdom in this place earlier, which was later on shifted to Haripur and thereafter to Baripada's Belgadia palace which today stands as a testimony to this historic-heritage sites. Panchpidh today comprises of a total five blocks viz; Karanjia, Jashipur, Thakurmunda, Raruan & Sukruli .It has a total of sixty gram panchayats & one NAC in Karanjia, the sub-divisional headquarter. The area is thickly populated by tribes like, santhal, bathudi, bhumija, kohl, gond and their major vocation is agriculture, cattle rearing & collection of minor forest products, as this region is a thickly forest land. This region is the last connecting point of Paandavas journey as they started from Raja Biraat's fort from Raibania to Shamibrukhya in Podadiha-Udala-than to Dubigarh-Itagarh in the similipal region then passed enroute in Sarat-Thakurmunda to Karanjia-Khiching otherwise famous as panchpidh region.

Many historians, researchers also earlier indicated about this, but the field study of this Fellow amply proves this point that from Raibania's Raja Biraat fort to Kichak's fort at panchpidh is a contigous route used by the pandaavas during their agayaatbasa after their defeat in the game of dice. The relics, antics, places of interests has amply proved this which during the field study found that – the Bhanja rulers like Kota Bhanj, Diga Bhanj, Rana Bhanj were fond of subtle art works which was promoted by them during their ruling years. In these period of 10/11 century the famous temple of Khiching was built up by the Bhanjas .At that time they were worshipping Buddha & Buddhist idol Abolkiteswara is found here in the temple. The remains of Biraat & Kichaka's fort was found in on the verge of complete extinction. The copper coins, plates and materials derived from the archaeological renovation few years back proves the point that – during Mahabharatian era the fort of Raja Biraat was found in the bank of river Bhandan and that of Kichaka's in the bank of river Khairi. Thus the two famous river 'khairi-bhandan' emerges from this region. Here also once the famous pet tigress khairi was found .The area was having the remains of some symbols, remnants of fort-walls, gadakhai (a watery circle built up by kings then from immediate enemy attack) and the Rajguru, Rani-gadhua pond also today stands to remind one the glory & grandeur of Mahabharatian era. This region was first excavated by Ley Tikkel during 1840 and thereafter the famous archaeologist Mr Begler visited it during 1874-76 when he found the famous temple and several stone curved idols were scattered everywhere and the initial attempt to collect these were takenup. Again in 1907-08 the Great Maharaja Shri Ramchandra BhanjDeo invited the archaeologist Nagendranath Basu who made some effort to realign the dilapidated region. Again in 1922-23 Maharaja Purnachandra BhanjDeo has assigned the revival work to Rai Bahadur Ramprasad Chandra, than the superintendent of Calcutta Museum who was instrumental in renovating, discovering, replacing and realigning many rare idols of ancient era curved with such architectural marvel which is difficult to get even today. This proves the love of maharaja's for fine arts- crafts and idol worshipping.

During the period of Maharaja Pratap Chandra BhanjDeo the 75 feet height temple of Khiching was realigned with ancient engravings by noted archaeologist Birbal Bose & Parmananda Acharya which took this new shape by 1940. This heritage piece have identical curvature with the famous Brahmeswara temple of Brahmeswarapatna in todays Bhubaneswar. These heritage sites gives evidences to several aspects then found by the patron –kings like Buddhism, Jainism and some rare forms of deities like, upward lingeswara, astabhuja Durga, ardha-narishwar, dancing Ganesha, apsaras, kartikeswara on mayura etc. The art-crafts of this famous Khiching temple is unique in the entire eastern India. Its presiding deity Khijingeswar is stated to be sitting naked on a corpse which except the pujak no one has seen nor permitted to witness since the days of Bhanjas.

The scholar-Fellow covered this famous heritage site along with few Engravings of statues, idols recovered from the debris of forts earlier on several occasions.

Benu Madhab Math : Paandava's place of worship

The exploration proceeded with the study of Mahabharatian era Matsyadesa with greater depths had connected the rich, resplendent region of nature from many historians, researchers of past who has some or other way worked in this region, on subjects other than this. The famous such persons were Nilamani Senapati, S.N. Sarkar, J.K. Sahu, Dr K.C. Panigrahi, Dr H.K. Mahatab, Janmejay Sahu, P.K. Dash to name a few who have depicted the place & region in their writings as a natures gift to world, but many have unable to draw such similarities of Mahabharatian era relics, except in an sporadic manner. As stated earlier the area in Raruan where Sahadeva & Nakula were looking after the cow-cattles of Raja Biraaat is a fertile land where crops grow immensely and the people were fond of eking out their living out of cattle rearing & grazing. Apart from a little distance of Biraat fort in Khiching comes the natures paradise, Similipal sanctuary. The Panch Paandavas were stated to be accompanying Raja Biraat during his 'mrigayaa' or hunting spree to this region. The Pandava's along with Sairindri or Draupadi were also accompanying Raja Biraat & his queen Sudeshna during their hunting and legend established that there is a BeniMadhb math-temple in this deep, dense forest zone and which probably they were worshipping. Because under what circumstances a Krishna or BeniMadhab temple was constructed by whom, & when is still an enigma. As the Paandavas were the sakha's and the worshipper of Lord Krishna, they have devoted their stay in worshipping HIM in this thick forest secretly. The area now is under reserve forest division of Similipal Authority. The Fellow also consulted with some elders about this and they had also substantiated this view that, when there is no population movement nor it falls on the usual human habitat route this might have built by the Paandavas.

Mahabharatian Heritage : Kichakeswari Temple

A number of cultural heritage sites dating back to Mahabharatian era as the local myths & tales depict the site and events. Raja Kichaka, the brother–in-law of famous Viraat-Raja of Mahabharata fame had his capital at Khijingkota, as known to historians and today it is famous as Khiching and its presiding deity called Kichakeswari. It was believed that Kichakeswari was the presiding deity of Bhanja kings and in a number of places the idols of Maa

Kichakeswari was found. In the Mayurbhanj palace itself, the western gate of the palace was the entry point of Maa Kichakeswari and it was closely worshipped by Bhanja kings exclusively by them only and outsiders were not allowed inside the temple. It is said that the temple Goddess was very effective (pratakhya)to the prayers of kings who inturn worship Her everyday and on some special occasions like, leading the armed forces on victory mission. The temple during the occasion of dussehra had witnessed large number of animal sacrifice including buffalo in its precincts which the royalty was fond of, to appease the deity. This palace temple was first opened to general public by Maharaja Pratap Chandra BhanjDeo during late 60's.Thereafter it was opened for all the time. The morning & evening worship bell of the temple reverberetes the whole palace precincts which several students used to witnessed as the palace was turned into a college by the Maharaja Purnachandra BhanjDeo. The temple has entry door like the Mughal era sculpture and its nata-mandap is like Hindu temple. The place where animals were sacrificed on tying on their heads has still withstood the time, engraving the blood of animal sacrifice, a saga of royalty.

The Kichakeswari Devi is the presiding deity of Bhanja kings till date and after the merger of Mayurbhanj state in 1949,its precincts was gradually diminished of celebrations like nitipuja, animal sacrifice etc for a longtime for dire want of funds and absence of royal patronage. But the present Maharaja Praveen Chandra BhanjDeo took a special interest in bringing back its past glory and accordingly reconstruction work begun and it has restored to its former glory. Now it performs its nitipuja and is open for public all the time. It has been covered with a number of photographs of this unique Mahabharatian era temple.

Region of Five : Paanchpidh

The Fellow continues with his study on the rare aspects of management of heritage sites dating back to Mahabharatian era in this matsya-desa region & more particularly in the Paanchpidh.-the Land of Five, in other words of Panchu-Paandavas. The mighty Paandavas spent their agyaatbasa in this Biraat & Kichaka Rajas region which is still an area of dense forest with mny mysterious places, signs, symbols, anecdotes dating back to Mahabharatian era. A major aspect of it is the area/region has always claim to be an important places since Mahabharatian era and is the legendary Matsyadesa,where shelters in disguise was extended to Paandavas by Biraat Raja of Mahabharat fame.The Paandavas lived on disguise in the form of cook, cowherd, musice teacher etc and served in the aja Biraat's kingdom. Todays Raruan & Jashipur blocks area captured,registers a number of anecdotes since Mahabharatian era. The Paandavas were very active & dynamic and scholars maintains that the area of Raruan & its people are very dynamic & active and their only means of livelihood is : agriculture & cattle rearing. Nakula, one of the paandavas had reportedly spent his major times tilling the land and grazing the cow,cattles in this particular area. this is believed by many elders and it was Nakula's ideals of promotion of agricultue & cattlegrazing, rearing that majority still works on his founded ideology in this area .The Mahabharitian scriptures also maintains that Raja Biraat had entrusted these duties to Nakula. The area & many of its region which we today called Raruan block has been partly ceded to Bihar & Jharkhand state. In 1949 when Sareikela & Kharswan region was given from ex-Mayurbhanj state, its major area or popularly those known as Mahabharatian heritage sites has been adjoined to neighbouring Jharkhand area.. There was a village named Benisagar which was earlier in Matsyadesa or Mayurbhanj but this heritage place Benisagar janpad (village) is now in Jharkhand state. The Mahabharat scriptures indicates that in a big pond in this village while Draupadi was taking bath her long jumbled hair in local language- beni was sink in this pond which was lateron given to the name of this village surrounded this area; hence the area is famous as Benisagar. This area further have another pond famous as ' Keshari Kund'. Nakula, Sahadeva, and others were usually taking bath in this pond. The citizens & society in this matsyadesa region had high regard & reverence and more particularly to Paandavas, because the localities here though didn't knew that these were Paandavas but they believed them to be something of special status and left this pond for their exclusive use; hence this pond was named as Keshari kund or Royal-pond. The locals still today elieves that deities use this pond hence they desist it from using it commoly. This pond & its adjacent area witnessed a Biraat -Mela or gala festival a the time of Makar sankranthi every ear, when thousands thronged to visit, worship the place by immersing in the pond. Those immersed on this pond in this particular day are stated to be reach the glory of their life & career. In other words those taking a dip on it would become the possessor of many unique quality & power. People here worship Maa Bhairavi- the deity and here sacrificial of animal is a taboo. He Raruan block is also otherwise popularly known as Nakulapidha-the region of Nakula. Many scholars claims that its ancient name on the versatile paandavas Nakula is largely a derivative of this region – Nakulapidha which also proves that unless Nakula was habitated it once, how this area cameup with this name in this thick tribal region.

Khiching : Cultural-Geograhic boundaries

This Paandavas infested region of Raruan in Panchpidh subdivision where the famous khiching temple stood. This heritage ancient temple's construction style is similar to Brahmeswara & Lingaraj temples of Bhubaneswar as its symmetry, aestheticness, beauty, curvatures reminds one the application of similar crafts in both these temples. Khiching- the region of Biraat & Kichaka where Paandavas used to hide themselves for a year was rippled with many tales,sites of Mahabharatian days,is a region to be preserved its heritage beauty but the management of cultural geographical boundaries has put this heritage cultural institution again into a fresh controversy. The issue starts when some locals found that the management responsibility of Khiching & its temples,museum is handed over to nearby Keonjhar district culture official department instead of Mayurbhanj, to which it belongs. The area is in the Mayurbhanj district and situated in Panchpidh which is nearer to Jharkhand on one side & Keonjhar on another side. Since generations the area, geography & heritage sites were under the direct control of Bhanja rulers which after the merger of Mayurbhanj state with Odisha found to be a district and this heritage site was managed under its culture officer. But how, why & when its management responsibility has been shifted to nearby district and under what context is beyond the understanding of all. Hence local population here agitated with such geographical transference of the govt. and even submitted memorandum to hon'ble Governor of Odisha. The Fellow also published the locals sentiments and urged the govt. to restore its status as before. Cultural & Heritage Institutions transgresses all geographical boundaries and belongs to all humanity and restricting it for a certain area, region or under certain control bound to generate heated sentiments.

Khiching was the ancient capital of Bhanja rulers where Mahabharat fame Biraat -gada(fort) was found to be stood once in the periphery of Bhandan river.The copper plate inscription, archaeological excavations and the artifacts found from this region proves this. Amidst thick jungles two rivers – khairi & Bhandan, the forts of Biraat & Kichaka was stood once as its remains were found for years after the merger of Mayurbhanj matsyadesa. In the year 1907-08 Maharaja Sri Ramchandra Bhanjdeo invited the noted archaeologist Nagendranath Basu from Kolkata to excavate the ancient sites which found several such heritage monuments then. Again in 1922-23 during the reign of Maharaja Sri Purnachandra BhanjDeo this site was again explored by Rai Bahadur Ramprasad Chandra, then superintendent of Indian Museum at Kolkata. Hundreds of ancient monuments, idols, artifacts were recovered from the damaged fort sites at Khiching and stored in the local museum here. Lateron Maharaja Pratapchandra BhanjDeo had entrusted the replication & renovation of famous Kichakeswari temple of Khiching by entrusting the work to archaeologist Paramananda Acharya which was completed by 1940. The 75 feet tall Khiching temple combines the ancient Mahabharatian art in numbers of its found idols such as : shiva, dancing Ganesha, Ardhanarishwara ,Asthabhuja Durga, Urdha-lingeswara etc. Khiching is one of the major shakti pitha' and people of all the religions, castes ranging from Brahmin, harijan, adivasi used to directly worship the deity. The community of stonework artisans is a rare community here on whose development the Scholar-Fellow has submitted a proposal to revive, popularize their unique art traditions to the newly formed State Institute for Arts & Crafts Development during this study. A writeup on the khiching of the scholar is also published highlighting several unique aspects of this Mahabharatian era heritage sites is given for better understanding.

Khijjinga Kotta Mandal & Modern Khiching:

The Importance of this heritage place could well be imagined when the Central govt. has included this place under its Rural Tourism Development Programme in Odisha alongwith seven other such heritage sites. The scholar-fellow launch a study on the trends and it is found that eight heritage-tourists spots like Konarka, Raghurajpur alongwith Khiching was extended with 4 Crore grant each of which would earmarked with 50 Lakhs of allocation to be spent for development of these heritage villages under Rural Tourists development Fund. But strangely except two projects – Konarka, Raghurajpur the rest village tourists programme was not even taken up even after four years of its sanction & there is chances that, the allotted amount may taken back by the Centre. When asked about non-expenses of the central govt. grant, the tourism department.has several reasons to offered like: the task was entrusted to INTACH and after two years they now back from this programme. Similarly the SIDAC-

State Institute for Development of Arts & Crafts was entrusted a part of this work but except issuing an advertisement for documenting stone arts curvings, it has so far not done anything concrete. These reasons have so far proved the inability in spending the huge grant allotted by Centre even after a lapse of four years, although stoneware artisans are facing fund crunch to improve their crafts & livelihood. As stated earlier, the adjacent village – Keshna nearest to Khiching is a village of heritage & crafts and requires fund support for its overall development but no such govt. programme has been launched although many craftsman's are leaving these traditional Art & crafts thus depriving the posterity about the rich heritageness of a place !

Many historians,researchers however subscribe to the view that,Kotta Bhanja is the founder of KhijjingKotta –one of the earliest known historical rulers of Bhanja dynasty of Khijjing. The copper-plate grants of Rama Bhanja mentions the year of 188 & 193 as an unspecified era,which probably was the 'Bhauma era'started in 736 & 929 AD. Thus it may be reasonably concluded that Kotta Bhanja-the grand father of Rama Bhanja flourished in the 9th century AD. Even he was restyled his name as 'Rajadhiraj' in the copper-plate grants. This Khijjing-mandala or modern Khiching is a region enriched in art, culture, aesthetics and exudes a rare charm of heritageness as one observes the archaeological remains, sites in this Mahabharatian era -Matsyadesa. British historians Lt.Tikkel & Beglar visited this region in 1240 & 1674 AD respectively. Khiching had originally a group of temples of which the main temple was that of Shiva - as the Bhanja Kings were Saivites and the Bhanja copper plate grants open with an invocation to Lord Shiva. Khiching was a 'Astayana Shaiva Kshetra' meaning Eight Linga's Place, were enshrined in eight temples. Today also one can see seven lingas at this place and the eighth one has been removed to Kesharibeda, the neighbourhood of Khiching. Three temples are still in sight at Khiching –Kutai Tundi is the oldest as its date of construction is assessed as 9th century AD. It was restored and reconstructed by Durbar Administration. The main temple, the presiding deity- Khijjingeswari has striking similarities with the temple of Brahmeswara of Bhubaneswar. This templ was buried under a mound on which stood a small brick temple of Khijjingeswari and an unfinished temple called Khandia- deula'. Maharaja Pratap Chandra & Purna Chandra Bhanj Deo took active steps to restore & renovate these oldest temples of Khiching under the supervision of Ram Prasad Chand alongwith Parmananda Acharya, Sailendranath Basu all archaeologists of repute.

The site museum at Khiching houses a large numbers of idols as per Hindu tradition found during excavation at different sites. The museum was organized in 1922 by R P Chand and is the largest Museum in Orissa with a collection of antiquities like – Stone sculptures, Lithic Implements, Beads, Pottery, Copper Plates & Sanads. After merger of Mayurbhanj state, a number of important artifacts from this museum was taken by Govt. of Odisha to state museum at Bhubaneswar, where it is now found and this museum left with few materials. Its management handed over to nearest Keonjhar district authorities has again earned the wreaths of locals and it is closed since last one & half years.

Though basically a Shaivaite establishments, the excavations during periods found large numbers of Sakta, Saura, Vaishnaba, Ganpatya tradition aplenty. It was observed that, there was fine blending of different religious cultures at Khiching under the royal patronage of Bhanja's. A major departure in Khiching's temples have – here no Mukhasala (frontage) or Natmandir is found. This same style was found in Brahmeswara at Bhubaneswar, Benisagar, Khekpatra, Anjan at Jharkhand, Bankura in Midnapore of West Bengal, Simdega in Bihar.

The Mahabharatian remains of two ancient forts – Biraatgarh & Kichakgarh (fort) were also found at Khiching few years back is now only houses the main temple. A Buddhist stupa with a casket and ashes was also discovered at Khiching ,as reported in the ASI Annual Reports in the year 1922 to 1925. Another very important aspect of Khiching was – it synthesise the Hindu & Adivasi culture,as here both the culture have merged. The temple is worshipped both by Hindu Brahmins & Adivasi-Bhuyan and it is always open for Hindus,Dalits,adivasis & every caste of people. Every year a big mela is held here during the Sivaratri festival when large numbers of pilgrims gather here to worship Kichakeswari and Nilakantheswara-Shiva close to the temple compound.

Keshna – derivative of Krishna'

A derivative from Krishna-Draupadi is the name of this village in this Paanchpidh region. The area is habitated mostly by stone curving artisans and its stone works are famous allover. The artistry on stone & its heritageness bears the testimony of a community which was famous for their artistry on stone. Draupadi was fell in love with these crafts, legends maintains. In ancient period the name of this area was Krishna-another name of Draupadi. Many villagers here feels that the present name of Keshna was largely derives from Krishna, otherwise why in a tribal region a village in the name of Draupadi caught the attention of villagers ,is stated to be due to Paandavas habitation once.

Similarly a little distance from Raja Biraat 's gada-fort there is also a village Pandurasila. In this area comparatively richer castes of kuber & gauda, a cattle rearing community one can found. The name of this village as Paandavsila was perhaps its earlier name which was lateron derivated as pandurasila. This Pandurasila or Pandavsila area is also popularly famous as Judhistirapidh, the eldest of Paandav as his superiority runs supreme in this region once, during their stay it is believed by local villagers, elders, researchers, historians. Interestingly numerous heritage sites, areas, villages, places clearly depict this region as Paandavas visited place once and it corroborates all the symptoms of Matsyadesa as described in Mahabharat.

The queen along with her group of beauty maidens & Paanchali used to took bath in this water reservoir, away from commonmen's sight.It was once during her bath that Draupadi lost her 'beni''(hair) in this lake hence this name-Benisagar. The lake situated in a sylvan surroundings even today, quite away from public gaze. The entire area is covered with tall Sal trees, the hallmark of Mayurbhanj forests, where one could find a big dam like facilities have been erected. Just infront of this water pond one found the excavations of a big fort is in the process since last three years.The excavated materials include stonewares, idols builtup of black-mugni stones akin to the stone crafts of khiching. A number of Shivalingas are also found in this excavations for which it led to believe that, perhaps after secretely taking bath, the queensfolk used to worship Shiva in this temple. The excavation is in progress presently by ASI, Ranchi circle and a number of idols have been recovered in this region. But sadly the area once habitated in Mayurbhanj is now in Jharkhand. The Fellow – asked about it and got the reply that,it was very much a part of Jharkhand.Hence the forthcoming generations might never believe that it was once a part of matsyadesa –due to this political & administrative divisions, leading towards cultural bifurcation.A big museum of ASI is also under construction process and house all those excavated rare ancient materials, recovered during these digging.The quality of bricks used in these excavated fort-temple is similar to that of Haripur & Khiching –rectangular in shape but thickness is less than todays bricks.The scholar-fellow took few snaps of this place ideal for meditation as tranquility rules here but was prevented by the ASI staffs, not to photographed as it is in progress. However three photographs was already taken which are given herewith.

Keshna – Abode of Krishna'

Draupadi whose other name is Krishna was assigned this village situated just four km.from famous khiching temple after one crosses Ghikhali village on the roadside.Both the side of road one could witness a number of stoneware artisans are busy in ripping the black mugni stones and out of it, they used to design various eyecatching stonecrafts-idols of different kinds,animals other household useable items are being forked out from these stones.Around 200 craftsman lives in this area alone of which 300 are households.Almost all the major adults are being trained to become a craftsman of stone artistry,but with days passed however their number started receding as new generes are opting jobs outside this traditional mode of earning. The villagers believed that their village keshna have a never ending supply of black-mugni stone out of which they used to earn their livelihood since generations. This black mugni stone is widely used in construction of famous khiching temple once.The villagers are proud of their crafts and is lamenting on the resource crunch in this stone arts & crafts.Few years ago a bank and a non-govt.orgn.has organized a workshop to build the capacities of stone crafts but greater efforts with funds to improve their skill, living is needed in this Mahabharatian site.Few photographs taken by the scholar of this area are given.

Biraat Sena- Mahabharatian relics

The existence of Biraat sena in this Mahabharatian famous matsydesa signifies that,Raja Biraat belongs to this region and interestingly a troupe called "Biraat sena" is in existence since long.They might have ascendants to the members of Biraat-sena(military) community.This sena very oftenraised the demand for a Biraat state for the community of Mahanta's who are neither tribals nor general- their physical features are sharp, tallsome of their habits are similar to local tribes & some are like general higher castes.They might have descendants of Biraat Raja's army,believes many,as a number of material evidence signifies that like their lifestyles, their taste for superior quality,their demand from exclusion from ST list before independence & now for reinclusion in this same list, their livelihood pattern mostly by cultivation, cow, cattle rearing & dependence on agriculture etc.

Bhima's Relics in Matsyadesa :

The Scholar-Fellow came across through few relics of Bhima - the Great Paandavas during their sojourn here in this Biraatdesa or Mahabharata fame Matsyadesa. Two relics are of much importance- Dhudhua in Kaptipada subdivision & Bhimkund near Thakurmunda under Karanjia or Panchpir (five-owners place) believed to be designated on the great Paandavas.

Dhudhua or Durudha is a hillock in Badkhunta in Kaptipada subdivision .Here is a waterfall whose sound goes to distant places. & Its name is derived from this sound – dhu, dhu. This hillock area is about five acres & in its south lies a pool of water which connects to the river – Gangahara. The pool from which this waterfall is known as 'Gauri-patta' containing a Swambhu-linga (nature made Shivalinga) wherein a big pool called 'Rohini-Kunda which witness a big mela every Baruni-day – during Shivaratri. In its east lies a hillock famous as 'Ghatsila. Here in a cave, the image of four armed goddess called Lakhai-handi is represented with a goat & a lion under her left and right feet .Few yards from this cave lies an oval stone which local here called 'Khuda-putuli' as it is popularly believed that the Great Bhima pressed his knees on this stone as the impressions are still visible on it. Ruins of three brick built temples was found earlier in three different places of Ghatsila earlier; which now is completely damaged. This ancient heritage site has been in a ruinous condition due to years of neglect by the local authorities opined a number of elders in this village.

Bhimkund

Another relics attributed to mighty Bhima is a large and deep pool of the Baitarani river in Thakurmunda region in Panchpir subdivision. The legend established that Bhima –

the second of Paandavas used to take his baths here in this place when lived in disguise in this Biraatdesa – stretched upto Kaptipada subdivision. Here the Baitarani river flows through a gorge in steps forming a series of picturesque rapids until it settles down in the pool called-Bhimkund or the Pond of Bhima .At one place the gorge is hardly four feet wide in winter; here the Baitarani disappeared underground by nature-walls giving a look of well protected pool. During Makar-sankranti , people in lakhs flock this place to take a bath in Bhimkund to wash their sins .This place has been gradually gaining importance with the celebrations of Bhimkund-mela every year which has popularized this spot as a major tourist-heritage zone, but more needs to be done to put this place in a proper tourist-maps of Eastern India.

Matsyadesa – A scholarly debate

The Fellow-scholar undertook grueling research on the various texts available regarding the exact position of Matsyadesa as described in the Mahabharat. A number of scholars, historians, researchers have believed- few other places as Matsyadesa apart from Mayurbhanj, but all ultimately fell to the theories, places, relics, anecdotes available in this region of Mayurbhanj. The Bengali Encyclopaedia describes that – the Mahabharat famous Matsyadesa as described can be found in Rajputana of Rajasthan and also in Bombay, Mednipur in Bengal or in the hilly regions of Mayurbhanj. However the testimonial-material available only in Mayurbhanj is akin with that of Matsyadesa and it gives this region as undisputed status as Matsyadesa of Mahabharat.

Some other historians maintains that Matsyadesa might have been based at any of these places:

North Biraat state – Bharatpur in Rajasthan.

South Biraat state – Mayurbhanj region.

East Biraat state – Shahbad in Bengal.

West Biraat state – Satara in Maharastra.

However such theories that Raja Biraat of Mahabharat fame might have his empire extended & expanded up to several regions of the country is believed to be vague. But the relics available in Mayurbhanj regions only qualifies it to be the perfect Matsyadesa as described in Mahabharat ideologically, geographically, historically and from all possible angles of scholarly pursuit.

The Mahabharat maintains that, the Paandavas along with Draupadi lived one year agayaatbasa (disguised living) quite away from Hastinapur or modern Delhi which must have been situated away from it. The Paandavas were stated to hided their weapons under a big tree known as Samibrukhya which can be found only in Mayurbhanj region as its description clearly indicated that Matsyadesa was a thickly forestry region. The Mahabharat further exemplify that, Duryodhana sent several envoys to locate the Paandavas during their agayaatbasa from Indraprstha-capital of Hastinapur but none of them was able to locate them; in other words it clearly points out that, matsyadesa was situated quite a distant place from Hastinapur. The common men & clergy of matsyadesa was unable to identify Paandavas, than the most admirable persona even during their agayaatbasa. Had the matsyadesa been situated nearest to Hastinapur it could have been easier for

Kaurava's to identify the Pandavas to break their agayaatbasa, which in other words clearly speaks that, matsyadesa was quite away, at a distant place from Hastinapur and was also cut off from Indraprastha politics then. In Biraat parva of Mahabharat it was stated that Judhistira the eldest of Paandavas first worshipped the presiding deity of Matsyadesa before entering in it, who was adorned with crown made up of peacocks broom as well as in its flag:

Mayurapichcha bataye keurangdadharini

Bharidebi jatha padma narayan panigraha - Biraat Parva- chapter 6, 8 sloka

Dhwajen sikhi pichchinamuchchitren birajse

Kaumaran bratamasthya tridivan pabitantwaya – Biraat Parva –chapter 6,

14 sloka

Tantra-chudamani further exemplifies that the names of the presiding deity of Matsyadesa was Ambika which is only found in Mayurbhanj region, giving credence to the only place as Matsyadesa. Even the origin of Maa Ambika place is also found in Deokund in the thickly mountaneous, forested belts of Mayurbhanj. As described in Mahabharat, here Draupadi used to made her juda (kasha/hair) in the right side of head before making visits to Rani Sudeshna as described in the 9th chapter 1-2 slokas of Biraat Parva:

Jugruhey dakshine parse mruduarit lochana

Basacha paridhayanko Krishna sumalinam mahat.

Draupadi used to bind her hair with flowers of malika, utpala, lotus & champaka which are abundantly found in the forest ponds of this region. The region have special leanings towards art, culture, music as Rajkumari Uttara had a special fascination for dance & music and Arjuna was her music teacher by bearing the name of Brihnnalla.

The Mahabharat describes that Kichaka was the mighty Senapati of Matsyadesa's Biraat Rajas and queen Sudeshna-Chitra, Rajkumar Dhananjay-Uttara,Rajkumari Uttarra and its frontier guards were known as baka & yakshya The language of matsyadesa was quite different from the prevalent languages of Hastinapur which unequivocally qualifies Mayurbhanj as Matsyadesa .Culturally & language wise the ideal positioning of Matsyadesa from Hastinapur must be above thousand miles away which it is.While disguised living the great Paandavas had identified themselves as Kanka, Ballava, Brihannalla, Granthika, Tantripala and Sairindhri. It is further contested that, when Paandavas were under a vow to keep their identities in disguise they must have resorted to these names inorder to hide their true identity whose affinity with names prevalent in this matsyadesa-Mayurbhanj region is found similar.

This region have abundant of horse & elephant population with the complete extinction of former & gradual diminishing of later.The major living of the inhabitants are from forest products collection, cow rearing, milking which one can found abundantly now also. The Mahabharat maintains that Duryodhana had attacked Matsyadesa by learning about its wealth & richness of cattles, milk and it has triggered the war against Matsyadesa through his associates like Trigartaraj Susharma & Angaraja Karna. The Biraat parva 16th chapter states that – the commander in chief of Matsyadesa, Raja Kichaka had plundered & defeated the Rajas of Anga, Banga, Kalinga and its kings were highly dissatisfied with such

heroic acts of Kichaka and wanted to teach Matsyadesa a lesson, had joined this war .The craving eye of Kaurava's about the rich animal wealth in shape of high yielding cow & milk has given the impetus for this attack to Matsydesa. This further testifies that the positioning of Matsyadesa was near to Anga, Banga & Kalinga states which only the Mayurbhanj's geographical location ideally provides. During the Budhadeva's journey of Budhattva-prachar, there were only 16 states allover India viz; Anga, Magadh, Kashi, Kosala, Bajji, Malla, Banse, Kuru, Cheti, Matsya, Panchala, Surasena, Asaka, Abnti, Gandhara, Kambauj. Budhadev visited all these states except Matsyadea to propagate his teachings. In other words Matsyadesa had strong Brahmanic & Vedic culture where Budhadhdeva even dared not to interfere to propagate Budhism. It is clear & established fact that Vedic & Brahmanic culture have been deeply embedded in Matsyadesa region as one can see in the present Mayurbhanj also. Another theory links that the Matsyadesa of Mahabharat fame was situated near sea and the Bay of Bengal is situated just few kilometers away from it and also surrounded in the areas upto, Chandipur, Paradip, Dhamnagar, Digha etc,
Another literary treasure Sadananda-saudagar- pala states that .after crossing Anga, Banga when one go towards Kalinga-rajya ,one encounters Biraat-rajya enroute. This describes the exact location suited to Mayurbhanj region only. From every scholastic angel it is now an established fact that-Matsyadesa's relics can only be found in today's Mayurbhanj as many existing materials points to this & here ends all the disputes that Mayurbhanj was the Matsyadesa of Mahabharat fame.

Cultural Heritage-Tangible & Intangible

The author have an opportunity to attend, interact a unique workshop organized by Indira Gandhi Rastriya Manav Sangrahalaya, Bhopal in Bhubaneswar this month where the theme was: protecting our cultural heritages. Many scholars addressed on the subject and this Fellow describes the unique cultural heritages of Mahabharatian era in the Matsyadesa of Mahabharata; today known as Mayurbhanj. He describes that there are two aspects to Cultural Heritages such as -Tangible Cultural Heritages (TCH) and Intangible Cultural Heritages (ICH).

The Tangible Cultural Heritages are consisting of: historical monuments, buildings and art objects. While Intangible Cultural Heritage has many forms : myths, legends, music, dance, crafts, technique, rituals which have passed on from one generation to another, Orally. Hence it is very important to study and document the hundreds of myths, legends, rituals, festivals, arts & crafts, communities, performing arts around & apart from the historical monuments. Because intangible cultural heritages is not only the heritage of those living in & around a monument area but also the common heritage of the human kind. So it is very important to document it in audio-visual and written formats. These Mahabharta era heritage sites & its surrounding areas have been preserving a huge number of Cultural Expressions over these years, but if left unattended, all precious heritage would be lost to oblivion and the future generation will never know its past glory, history and cultural store house. The Fellow stress on the needs of exploring further that how the Intangible elements have been contributing for development of society.

BHANJA - VIGNETTE
MANAGEMENT OF HERITAGE ART CULTURAL INSTITUTIONS
SECTION: B
BHANJA VIGNETTE
Neglected Heritage sites

This Matsyadesa houses several relics, monuments, anecdotes, sites, heritage spots in its interior Similipal biosphere region which is a great tourist place dating back to Mahabharatian era,it is believed.The modernization process of this route by earmarking few crores of central grant and surrounding walls restoration is a appreciative step.

There are huge neglected heritage sites allover this Mahabhrtian era fame Matsyadesa or modern Mayurbhanj on which a vivid documentation with photographic details have been attempted.The Nrutyakothi or dance palace of kings on which a photo documentation was made used by the kings but it is found that this old heritage building of around 1800 AD has been razed to ground by administration and in its place the newly constructed district treasury building has been erected.This heritage building was in very dilapidated condition and was a den of antisocial elements,criminals as it was in an abandoned state by the ruling family, the criminals very often hide the smuggled goods such as timber and other articles. Few persons have encroached the frontage of this heritage building site and have raised jhopdi, dhaba etc for which the administration receives a number of complaints and it was razed to ground and the new district treasury building have comeup. Interestingly the district administration found it more appropriate to raze it to dust instead of salvaging its ruinous condition to its former glory as a place of tourists interests before the process of its restoration.A local orgn has since last few years trying to restore it to its architectural designs and communications with few authorities were made but this heritage building of Bhanja's is found to be disappeared from the region of Matsyadesa.

Another visiting place is Gouranga Temple situated nearby the Mayurbhanj palace which was built by Maharaja Jaganath BhanjDeo between 1600 to 1643 AD.This historic shrine has special mention in the history of Mayurbhanj as during the visit of Shri Chaitanya Mahaprabhu this temple was built to commemorate his visit to this region.

The famous Brahmo Samaj temple built with the patronization of Mayurbhanj Maharaja Sri Ramchandra BhanjDeo who has been highly influenced by noted Brahmo Samaj founder Sri Keshab Chandra Sen of Bengal.This Brahmo temple has been rebuilt after efforts were takenup by this author in highlighting it in media.

Maharani Laxmikumari Dharmasala

The ancient heritage building of Maharani Laxmikumari Dharmasala near Sri Jaganath temple was built by Maharaja Sri Ramchandra Bhanj Deo during 1905-06 for the short stay of tourists, devotees visiting to this temple area, as this area have several deities & temples. Laxmikumari Devi is the beloved wife of Maharaja who died of malaria, than a dreaded disease & in her memory this dharmasala was built which used for free bording, lodging for short stay tourists for many years. After the merger of Mayurbhanj state the state endowment department have taken charge of its maintenance and first it imposed a tariff than increase it until 2003 when the MP Birbhadra Singh has funded this dharmasala & changed it into sadbhavana mandap by defacing, reconstructing it from behind its back, as a result it has lost its past ambience of its heritage grandeur. Today it has completely converted into a commercial centre and needs high payments for the its users. During Maharaja's time it was a practice that they built rest houses every 9 miles corresponding to 12 km distance which are today neglected, dilapidated & become the centre of all antisocial acts. Speedy takenup of reconstruction of these ancient rest houses is the need of the hour. One such covered here is Nichuapada built during the Bhanja's period.

Maa Dwarsuni Temple

One of the most ancient deity is Maa Dwarsuni believed to be appeared enroute on the ghat of national highway no 5,6.Earlier She was worshipped under a banyan tree and every passersby vehicles stop for a while to paid obeisance to Her. It is a common belief that those stop to worship Her reach their destination smoothly & safely.The deity is worshipped not by Brahmins but by non-brahmins called as Dehuri's.Today a temple has comeup in & around Maa Dwarsuni or Goddess of Doorway and become a tourists spot as seen from the photofeature.

Haripur Fort

The legendary neglected heritage site Haripur was the capital of Matsyadesa Mayurbhanj during 1400 AD after the Sultan Ferozshah Tughlaq destroyed its ancient capital in 1361 AD at Khijjing-kota or todays Khiching. Several historical sources pointed out that Haripur was the capital of Bhanja's during 1300 – 1630 AD. Few other historians are of the opinion that, it was founded by Harihara Bhanj during 1322 saka era or 1400AD. Some other historians maintains that it was founded by Harikrishna Bhanj who ruled during 1464 to 1491. Haripur or earlier Hariharapur fort is also popularly known as Bankatigada i.e,fort built after clearingup forests, which is at present in ruins and three temples – Rasikarai or Rasikaraj,Radhamohan,Sri Jaganath are found in its ruinous zone.The temple of Rasikarai today also stands with its early splendour with the Archaeological Survey of India's (ASI)effort. Most of the art & architecture depicts the influence of Vaishnavism with high degrees of Mughal era architectural style.This fact was indicated by many early researchers which has been established by this fellow-author during the study of certain architectural designs of Mughal era.Very near to this place in eastern India's Murshidabad the Namakharam Mahal (traitors palace)stands today whose designs are very much synonymous with Haripur fort & its heritage buildings. The one common factor between these structures are the rectangular shaped bricks whose thickness is about 1.5 inch but its length & breadth are about 18 & 8 inches respectively. The dome of Haripur fort today houses Rasikraj, Jaganath temples alongwith the most ruinous structures of Radhamohan temple. The ASI has actively took steps to revive the lost splendour of these two ancient temples & able to reproduced the bricks exactly in shape & size of those era and have facelifted two of the temples to a major extent to its former glory. No deities are presently there but the temples bears the testimony of the great tastes of Bhanja rulers & their love for aesthetics.The temple of Radhamohan situated within the fort zone is in dilapidated condition and no effort was taken by ASI to reinvent it. Similarly there is an underground structure equivalent with two big halls which the locals call the Cell to keep dreaded criminals. Some others are also of the view that, these were used by queens for their personal upkeep purposes. Whatever its uses were, the last excavation made by ASI during 80's in this area has also invented these two halls which also put an enigma before all. Apart from these, there are several tombs, pillars, domes, walls which silently depicts the rich cultural heritages of the erstwhile Bhanja rulers of Mayurbhanj. These several spots have either not completely excavated by ASI or remain halfdone with lack of political, historical interests & the dearth of funds.The ASI is gradually building an encompassing compound wall alongwith its main gates & other such relics carefully to reinvent the past magic of Haripur,the former capital of Bhanja's famous as Matsyadesa during the Mahabharat era. There are two big ponds near this fort zone,one of which keep water round the year -the big one but the more deep one remains always dry except few months during rainy season. Locals attributes it to the curse of Maharani for this unique phenomenon. This place was flourished to its full during Jaganath Bhanj who married to the daughter of Gajapati Raja of Puri, Shri Prataprudradeva. Once Pratrudradev was journeying for piligrimage to Brindaban via Ramchandrapur enroute Mayurbhanj and suddenly fell ill and breathed his last here. He asked his son in law to make arrangements for his 'aaradhyadeva' Shri Jaganath and accordingly the Raja made arrangements of this Jaganath temple.The village where Gajapatiraja Prataprudradeva breathed his last was renamed after him as Pratap-pur & bears the testimony of those era. The Jaganath, Balabhadra, Subhadra idols are being worshipped in the Pratappur Jaganath temple instead of Haripur fort temple, when Kalapahad attacked this region.

Sri HariBaladevjew Jagannath Temple

The major cultural & also spiritual festival of odisha is Ratha-yatra or popularly known as Car festival allover and Matsyadesa, Mayurbhanj's place comes next after Puri since tha Maharja of Mayurbhanj-the Bhanja's have donated graciously for the observance of niti-puja with grandeur. The HariBaladevjew temple otherwise known as Sri Jagannath temple is dating back to 1575 AD and built by Maharaja Shri Baidyanath BhanjDeo. A peep into its landed property invested since the times of Bhanja's with khata no,plot no,area,mauza villagewise are too vast to be documented here.However it surfaces during the course of this study that thousand acres of Haribaldevjew temple land property has been dispapppeared from the record of rights registers of the deity, questioning the vast mismanagement of temple land administration.

The issue was raised by the author and the chief minister call for a meeting to recoup the Jaganath temple land from the encroachers. The problem with the lands are: they officially belongs to Jaganath temple to be enjoyed by its sevayats but with each passing years the new generations have devised ways & means to record it in their personal names striking the names of Lord Jaganath,which has created a number of conflicts,litigations as well as disruptions in the niti-puja of Lord Jaganath.Perhaps allover the country people donate to God but except very few,in this land of odisha many found to be record the properties of temple in their own names.Similarly the issues of ornaments given by the Maharajas of Mayurbhanj to the temple has also found to be disappeared from its treasury causing much furore in the media which has also been takenup specially by this author.

Heritage Air fields

The heritage air fields evolved, developed during erstwhile kings of certain feudatory states which now comes under newly curvedout districts. One such famous is Amarda Air strip or field developed by Britishers during IInd world war 1939-1945. This air field is presently located in the exstate of Mayurbhanj under Rasgobindpur block.Hundreds of acres were donatedby former Maharaja on which facilities for landing of eight airplanes at a time have been developed.Its runways have eight such pads on which airplanes engaged in IInd world war came to took rest here. The airbase has many undergrounds, pillars, walls, rest shades out of which severals have been razed to ground by encroachers in absence of proper maintenance. Hundreds of acres of its lands though found to be record ed in govt but possessed by outsiders as such little protection was meted to this heritage site as a result the area has been encroached by many and since 2004 construction of palatial buildings by few have surfaced in this protected zone.It is the only airstrip available to eastern India under the Chandipur DRDO & Kaleikunda airbase and used as a base for landing dignatiries like President,Pimeminister etc.The other heritage air bases are at Rajaloka, Fatehgarh, Jharsuguda, Barbil, Dandbose-to name a few in the entire state apart from Bhubaneswar aerodrum.

Jubilee Library

Another heritage site is Jubilee Library-a name given by Maharaja Sri Ramchandra BhanjDeo which commensurates the jubilee year of the Empress Queen Victoria, London & designed in unique British style.The

Maharja initially setup a library (pathagara) in his royal palace & in 1893-94 he expands it to the Jubilee library and also the founder President till his last. The Maharaja has formed an autonomous committee to manage its affairs which is still continuing.This heritage building is also known as Sri Ramchandra Pathagara since 1901. Now its entire area is surrounded with boundaries and has possessed rare books, journals in its collections.Lateron the management of this pathagara has been taken up by culture department, govt. of odisha.

Lulung & Sitakund

Another heritage as well as tourist site is Lulung & Sitakund- a perennial stream exists & attracts thousands of tourists ,also the entry point of Similipal sanctuary.It also houses many Mahabharatian era site,relics and now the department of tourism have a tourist bunglow here for the stay of visitors round the year.

Raghunathjew Shrine

There are two famous heritage shrines Raghunaathjew- one at Jahipur and another at Baripada.The regular theft of ornaments given by Bhanja rulers and embezzlement of landed properties of the Jews donated by Maharaja's as niti-puja today are facing major crisis which needs to be replaced with more vigilant approach as well as dedicated sevayats.

Nagra-bhadi or Nagada House

Nagra-bhadi or Nagada house, a particular instrument with a roaric sound is an old heritage building situated infront of the famous Jaganath Temple of Baripada built during 1575 AD by Maharaja's of Mayurbhanj.It contains a thrre storied layers of nagda players in this mansion when the Lord Jaganath's morning, noon & evening aarti begans.The tradition of nagra worshipping continued till seventies and during eighties it was on the wane. This famous tradition of nagra and their players came to a close in absence of patronization and today this heritage building has been encompassed with several encroachments as number of shops have denigrated its monumental value.Thus families ekingout their living out of this nagra-playing tradition are a vanished lot.

Bhudhara- Chandi Heritage temple

The Nilgiri fort range has a unique temple heritage site of Maa Bhudhara-Chandistated to be appeared from the earth itself during 15th century under a neem tree. As the deity had appeared from under the earth She is named Bhudhara. The temple depicts around 106 images of different deities depicting from Mahabharat era. It was built during 1905 by the Nilgiri Raja ShyamSunder Mardaraj.It is one of the major neglected but famous Shakti-pithain northern odisha in most dilapidated consition and needs immediate patronization.

Bhanja's worshipper of Bishnu cult

A 15th century dilapidated Bishnu temple came to limelight in the village Padmapur-Deuli in Jharpokharia area which speaks the Bhanja's devotion towards Bishnu-Narayana. Infact if one goes through the geneology of Bhanja dynasty one would found that some of the Bhanja's were Shaivites, some Vaishnavites & some belongs to Jaganath cult, whereas some, Chaitanyaties-followers of Shri Chaitanyadev Mahaprabhu. Such cult worshipped configured the royalty for certain period at a certain time.The said Bishnu idols recovered from the underneath, is about 3 feet 10 inch which epitomized the four arms-chaturbhuja posture of the deity with sankh, chankra, gada, padma. Noted researchers of this area are of the view that, the name of the village Padmapur-Deuli probably stems from this Bishnu idol. The village is surrounded with six Brahmin- sasans which confirms the worship in the Bishnu temple.

Mayurbhanj Textiles

Mayurbhanj Textile Mill setup By Durbar Administration during Bhanja's in this underdeveloped backward region which started production in 1943 with the installation of imported machineries from England and was a profit making factory until the merger of Mayurbhanj .Thereafter its shares & stakes were transferred to govt of odisha which manged its affairs till 1960. But the state govt.mananged public limited company with an authorized share capital of 6 lakh and paidup capital of 2.50 lakh, it has 62% of the share. Its finished products on hosiery items have wide local as well as national markets outside odisha & especially in kolkata, Mumbai. But the state govt appointed boards mismanagement has put this heritage factory into a grinding halt from 1962. In 1992 the then chiefminister Biju Patnaik gave 10 lakh package for its revival but there was lockup in the factory due to mismanagement.All the trainees mostly tribals lost their skills, many have lost their jobs and the factory's 109 acres of valuble land adjacent to it attached by Bhanja rulers during 40's become bone of contention for the future royalty of the dynasty. The brother of Bhanja kings having two wives one is from Bastar state & another from this locality having different stakes on this property and thus a legal court battle was ensued between them. However taking advantage of long years of absence of Maharani of Bastar the local descendants have started selling the valuable 109 acres of Textiles land to different persons since 1979.As a result the area encompassing this textiles has been completely disappeared and only its boundary walls have been enveloped from all sides to this heritage zone. This entire heritage zone today is found to be completely overshadowed by private houses, sold illegally by one of the descendants of Lalsaheb Prafulla Chandra BhanjDeo .Thus the entire heritage Textiles buildings, lands, machineries have all sold to different parties and except this boundary walls nothing is available on the site.

Belgadia Palace

The palace of Bhanja rulers situated in the middle of Baripada town sprawling across 25 acres of land situated amidst thick greenary. The present day population have seen the rise & fall of many rulers starting from Sri Ramchandra BhanjDeo to Purna Chandra Bhanj, Pratap Chandra Bhanj, Pradip Chandra Bhanj and now Pravin Chandra BhanjDeo, who usually stays at Kolkata but often came to this ancient palace, the glory of Bhanjas. The palace is managed by a team of staffs which put a bar on taking snaps of this palace without permission of royalty. The Fellow thus undertook only the photos of entrance royal gate of this palace along with the stonewalls built around this famous Belgadia palace – a heritage site of Bhanjas and prefers to wait for the royalty to arrive from Kolkata when the necessary permission to photo-document the palace would be made in detail.

Budha-Raula Mahadev Matha

Another heritage dimension of art & culture is Budha-raula Mahadev. The Mahadev was appeared after a sadhu sat here on 'dhuni' for years in the river bank of chipat. Locals here call the Mahadev as Budha-raula.This is a famous

Shiva temple as well as Matha which has been renovated with ministers local area development fund of 5 lakh way back to 2002. A dhuni-ashram site, temple, storage and main temple was renovated by few local enthusiast on this Bhanja rulers heritage buildings.

Mayurbhanj Palace: A site of Royal heritage

The Bhanjas were lover of grandeur and style and it is said that the Mayurbhanj Palace built by Sri Ramchandra Bhanj was designed on the line of Britains Buckingham Palace. This royal palace was one of the best testimony of Bhanja royalty as it sprawls across few acres having dome, structures and swimming pools, temples everything. The Durbar Hall was one of the magnificient arena where royalty of different states used to gather during important occasions like famous Mayurbhanj Chhau festival, Makarsankranthi or any other festivities when the real grandeur of royalty speaks to people. This palace was donated by Maharaja Purna Chandra Bhanj during 50's for opening of a College in his name which still bear it today by giving access to common men to know about the royalty of Bhanjas. The durbar halls have been converted into classrooms, the Maharani swimming pool has been redesigned as library of the college and many such changes have been embedded in its walls & structures. However this bears a unique testimony to the Bhanja heritage.

Makar-sankranti mela- A unique heritage rites of local tribes

The famous Makarsankranti mela is observed allover Mayurbhanj which since the State-period to till date is a major state festival. The local tribals like santhals, bathudi, bhumij came to river Balanga to exonerate their dead men's bone on the river, a festival which continue for a week. Similar Makar festival was celebrated at Samibrukhya as described earlier and it was also witnessed many local cultural teams, unique to this region.

Talsari – Tourism zone in need of patronage

This tourist spot is situated bordering Digha, having unraveled famous spots such as, Bhusandeswar Shiva, Chandeneswar, Basuli, Astasambhu of Dahmunda, Baradeuli, Jaganath temple of Kamarda, a tourism growth plan of 80 crore since long is pending due to political rampage. Half a dozen politicians have assured many things so far but this unique heritage tourist zone in Bhograi-Talsari sea beach is still languishing amidst wanton funds & patronage. A peep into this unique zone.

Creamation-Places or Personal Holdings

An alarming trend noted by the scholars that creamation-ghats are fast encroached by persons, builders in collaboration with govt. officials into converting dwelling places illegally. Several such crematorium- ghats locally known as Shamsans are being encroached fast by several illegal occupants .This has shrinked the serenity in the cremation area and increased the pollution & other hazards. Samsan-ghats are even not free for departed souls which is a major trauma of modern times. The scholar-fellow also given his initiatives of 2001 while protesting such acts by few of a particular community and also how he was treated by causing injury & harm while working for this common interest.

Deokund – A major shakti-pitha

There are 51 shakti-pitha allover and the famous ones are: Jwalamukhi in Kangra valley of Himachal Padesh where the 'tongue'of Mata Shakti was fallen.Katyani' in

Brindaban,where the 'hair' was fallen.Kanyakumari,where the 'shoulder & back of mata' was fallen and 'Kamakhya'mandir in Guwahati of Assam where 'Shakti's 'yoni' was fallen.These four pitha's are major shaktipitha's alongwith 47 other places where the pieces of Mata Shakti was stated to be fallen after She was torn into pieces by an angry Shiva-Her husband. Deokund is another place in this matsyadesa region where part of the 'yoni' of Mata was believed to be fallen and it is the origin place of Maa Ambika-as shakti is known here. The Brahmin told that before the rajasankranti – a major festival in odisha during the month of June. The temple which is situated amidst the sylvan surroundings of Similipal's region and much above the land level on a rocky mountaneous range, with a high power current water fall, the temple closes for four days,as the water is found to be "red' during these days.In other words it is a 'rajaswala' period of "Mata or yearly cycle of period. During these days all sorts of worship in this pitha is stopped. The place is an ideal spiritual place where tourists and devotees flock together in large numbers.A two hour drive from headquarter Baripada, this place is now having good motorable roads courtesy PMGSY and lot of improvements in road infrastructure has been developed. One needs to ascend around hundreds of stairs builtup on rocky stones to reach this pitha where Maa Ambika is believed to be originated. A mysterious atmosphere along with mythical surroundings has given rise to many folklore and exudes a rare spiritual mystical charm here where once Lalsaheb Prafulla chandra BhanjDeo ,the brother of king used to come & practise his 'tantra'sadhana,wrote Devi tantra Sadhana, extensively. Maharaja Shri Ramchandra Jayanti politicized

The Maharaja Sri Ramchandra BhanjDeo's birthday 17 Dec was observed by the admn.& people alike every year,but the ugly politicization of Jharkhand leders have put a bandh call on this very day which resulted allover unrest on some flimsy grounds.Intellectuals of the region have criticized the jharkhandi's for their such acts detrimental to regional interests.Number of incidents reported from allover due to this unrest.A number of political leders alongwith some local mediamen have degenerated this auspicious birthday of Maharaja into a political gimmick.

Similarly the scion of Maharaja Sri Pravin Chandra BhanjDeo alongwith Rajmata Bharati Rajlaxmi Devi was misbehaved by a MVI in Laxmannath checkgate-the border in odisha-Bengal when despite the Maharaja's identifiction statement, the officials said- I donot know any Maharaja,I am the Maharaja of this place'.This led to serious administrative & public debate about the discourteous behaviour of certain employees who are so eager to earn bribe that in their lust they even unable to recognize man of royalty.This surely is a fall in virtues & display decay in our culture.

Kamardiha Matha-A ruinous heritage site

The Maharajas of Mayurbhanj were fond of establishing Matha-temple cum-rest sheds during their tenure and many such matha's are fast disappearing with the modern hotel-culture'.Khunta-Kamardiha matha situated in Rasgobindpur block is one such neglected heritage site.Its massive landed property situated at Baunsatofa, kamardiha, khunta, panchmania, jharia, Majnadiha, Dhansole,Bhandabhati are now illegally captured & even recorded officially this was disclosed during the field-study of the scholar.A number of temple-matha management officials are involved in such illegal transfer of deity's landed property which has been unearthed during this visit.A number of locals have demaned the restoration of deity's property in the name of khunta-kamardiha matha as before.The matha,it is said that, the biggest royt in this entire region whose cultivation & yielding of crops runs to lakhs every year.However the rampant irregularities have deprived the matha & its deity as well as dependants tenants,the accrued benefits by the scholar along with photographic details of -a rare heritage site since long.

Kakharua Baidyanath: Cultural heritage of Bhanja Dynasty The study of one of the most ancient heritage site, divine institution believed to be directly blessed by Lord Kakharua Baidyanath, incarnation of Lord Shiva. According to popular prevalent folklores of this region there are a number of anecdotes associated with this traditional cultural heritage institution which become instrumental in setting up of this rich divine, tourists & worship spot. This famous heritage spot is in Manatri,36 km from the headquarter of Mayurbhanj and is situated on the river Gangahaar. Once the Puri-Gajapati Raja was suffering from deadly leprosy disease and during his pilgrimage and sojourn near this site, he was instructed by Lord in his dreams that Lord Shiva is under the pumpkin (kakharu, locally known) tree and he digged it and found Shiva linga inside the river Gangahaar and started worshipping. During heavy rainy days, the shiva-linga was inundated with flood waters; showing this, the pujak fall prostrated and since that year, the river turn its course, leaving a trail of water streams known as kundi on which this cultural heritage site has been erected. The most significant part of this heritage site is, all the Shiva-lingams allover are worshipped by bel-patta; here Kakharua Baidyanath Shiva is being worshipped with both tulsi & bel leaves. As it was appeared beneath a kakharu leaf tree, it is popularly known as such.

According to another popular folklore, once a cowherd boy was guarding the cows and found one of its milchcow is not in the group. He made frantic search of this cow and found it in the bank of river Gangahaar where it was standing near a kakharu leaf tree and milk was pouring from its body. The next day he also found that this partcular cow is regularly going to that particular spot and sprinkling milk underneath this kakharu tree. He narrated this entire incident to villagers who came and digged the place and found Shiva linga, which later on led for establishments of today's famous Kakharua Baidyanath Pitha. A nuimber of villagers had donated each three maan (around a bigha) of land for this pitha for which this area is known as Manatri meaning three- mana and lateron Bhanja Kings were instrumental for constructing this heritage site structure.

This heritage-cultural temple was probably built during later 14th & early 15th century AD according to few other scholar- historians, when the famous Puri Gajapati Raja Kakharua Dev and in Mayurbhanj Maharaja Balabhadra BhanjDeo was ruling this region. During the visit of Puri-Gajapati the construction of this temple might have begun. Another mythology holds that during 1556 AD it was built by Mahaaja Baidyanath BhanjDeo who was also the builder of famous Shri Hari Baladev jew(Jaganath) temple in Baripada. The fact is historically verifiable as the structures, domes, natamandir of Kakharua pitha are largely identical with this Jagannath temple and it is quite different from usual shiva temples. He established the idols of Lord Jagannath in this pitha hence an ideal place of worship for Hari (Vishnu) & Hara (Shiva). Everyday the temple includes a kakharu as its prasaad and despite a shiva-pitha it usually observes all the festivals of Jagannath temple with equal fervour & grandeur like ratha-yatra, devasnan, jhulan, dolapurnima. But the most important & unique festival here is Maha Shivaratri which usually observed for a fortnight every year with lakhs of devotees thronging from allover. This rich heritage site & temple have hundreds of acres of land engaged by Bhanja rulers for the smooth management of deity & temple with grandeur. Baba Kakharua Baidyanath is surrounded with Shri Loknath, Shri Maliknath, Shri Kundanath, Shri Barahnath, Shri Swapneswarnath apart from Mahveer-Hanuman, Maa Durga.

Its raw flavour during Maha Shivaratri and the most scenic part is the appearance of deity from the river bed. A number of photo-essays on this site is given herewith exclusively to depict the unique heritageness of this place.

Manatri & Kuradiha Garh

In this region two famous garhs, forts viz, Manatrigarh, Kuradihagarh and Mangobindpur-garh were stated to be existed. Once Manatrigarh was existed near Manatri village stated to be built during Maharaja ShriDam Chandra BhanjDeo which once was a flourishing area. Mangobindpur garh was stated to be established by Gajapati Kakharua Raja's dewan- Gobinda Bidyadhara who after killing the former had captured this fort. The remains of both these garhs, heritage sites are hardly available today except their wall-edges at one or two places which simply reminds one of their ancient importance. Similarly kuradihagarh is situated enroute to Manatri-Baripada which today has converted into a rest house with few addition & alteration. This fort has four big halls and the Bhanja kings were stated to play dice in this place. Maharaja Damodara BhanjDeo took shelter during Marhattas invasion which the later have desecrated and made a heap of bricks in village kuradiha.

Baruneswar Mahadev

This famous site is situated in a spring called Baruni and known as such. This place of worship was built by Lalsaheb Prafulla Chandra BhanjDeo, the younger brother of Mmaharaja who was engaged himself with number of occultism, tantra etc and used to meditate most of the time in this serene place. Lord Baruneswara Mahadev is the presiding deity to this gateway to heavens; as the famous Hindu cremation place known as Barunighat exist just by its side, which was setup during Maharaja Shri Ramchandra BhanjDeo and later on renovated for the use of humanity since then.

Sarada Mandir : abode of Lalsaheb's

The Sarada-mandir is one of the heritage temple situated in the precincts of Lalsahebs – the king's brothers. It was treated as a personal temple of Lalsahebs till merger and after it was opened for general public. Maharaja's built several temples –many for personal worshipping & few for public entry & worshipping. Jwalamukhi, Purnachandra, Maa Kichakeswari - all were built around the protected premises of Maharaja's which after the kingship, was opened for public wroshipping. Maa Sarada temple is the personal temple of Lalsaheb Nirmal Chandra BhanjDeo family who carry all its responsibilities-from maintenance to establishment. The area of Maa Sarada temple is later on built with a hotel- Grand, Kichaka, a cinemahall - Roxy and a cycle stand. The income from these establishment go for the development & niti-puja of Sarada temple. Navaratri is being celebrated here with gaiety. Its adjacent areas are covered with shop rooms and its periphery management is important with regard to its heritageness.

Saras-kshetra of Lord Jaganath

Lord Jaganath is the deity allover people worship and number of temples were constructed apart from Puri & Baripada and one such is Lord Jaganath of Saraskshetra, situated at Saraskona. Around 40 km from district headquarter Baripada, Saraskona is situated bordering Bengal & Jharkhand and became a constant headache for administration with regard to maoist & Naxalites infiltration over these years. Bad road condition alongwith local groupism mindsets has put this Saraskshetra - Saraskona as one of the most law & order troubled area in Mayurbhanj. Recently the delimitation commission has declared Saraskona as a separate assembly constituency & for the first time it is being represented in assembly and people hope for its overall development. Saraskshetra-Saraskona have revived this Jaganath temple in 2002 with the active involvement of Puri Gajapatiraja and the temple is now built with modern styles .Its adjacent haat gives royalty from its income to the temple & the collection from temple-hundi.. The area is completely neglected & its revival with Jaganath culture has put some sort of religiosity with regard to the lawless elements, disturbing peace in this area.

Chahla-Heritage tourist site in rampage

The Maharaja's of Mayurbhanj were lovers of nature,

hunting & Similipal plateau provides them with an ideal site of thick forest amidst natural beauty. The Maharaja's have built Chahala Forest rest House (FRH) where during winter months, they used to come for rest, relaxation & hunting .With years passby several FRH were also built by them at scenic locations like – Nwana, Gudgudia, Barhakamuda, where forest beat house alongwith these luxury rest houses were built by them. Lateron used by tourists on payment. The Chahala FRH- the most oldest heritage house was ransacked recently by hooligans threatening tourists not to invade their abode. They had damaged part & parcel of this heritage house which the media termed as acts of maoist. Whatever the menace is - this heritage house was disfigured due to such rampage whose upgradation into former royal status is found to be a difficult job.

Astamprahari-baadi-pala culture –on wane

The region interlinked with Bengal, Jharkhand has also express its unique culture of baadi-paala & astam-prahari. In baadi-paala the villagers contributed cash, rice and young girls recite literary creations of Madhusudan Roy, Radhanath Ray, Fakirmohan's poem (kaavya) & also Bhagavata, Mahabharata. In astam-prahari culture, a troupe of kirtaan singers used to play khol, kirtaan in a turnaround way by installing Narayan. This round about ways of reciting God's glory for days together without any breaks in between, is said to be a gift of Mahaprabhu Shri Chaitanyadev's culture. Shri Chaitanyadev of Goudia matha in Bengal have highly mesmerized people in this region and round the year- be it chaitra or baisakha purnima till the end of Raas-purnima- this is evident allover, round the year. The peculiar character of this culture is —whatever the condition or situation is, be it flood, drought or rain, winter it has always propelled people in the tribal villages also to prepare such cultural fiesta off & on to remind the glory of great ancient heritage once this region bears. This culture of late although threatened by the invasion of new entertainment culture of cinema, TV has again revived in most gigantic manner by the simple villages folk and largely attributed to them.

Matsyadesa-Mayurbhanj: A Cultural Fiesta

The contiguous culture of Mahabharat fame Matsyadesa-today's Mayurbhanj is the birth place of many cultures, traditions & languages. The Santhali language took birth on the soil of Mayurbhanj & its propounder Pandit Raghunath Murmu. The renaissance in education was caused by Ravenshaw College established at Cuttack; so also the SriRamchandra Bhanj Medical college- these were the early landmark to augment new vistas in development by the Maharaja's of Mayurbhanj. Enlightened, highly educated, the benevolent kingship of Bhanja rulers in this Mahabharat fame Matsyadesa is a landmark in every direction. Maharaja's of Mayurbhanj had extend massive funds support for compilation of Oriya Bhashakosh-which was named as Purnachandra Oriya Bhashakosh in eight parts and is considered a treasure of Oriya language. The Bhanja rulers had donated around 8 lakh to Utkal University when it was first setup in 1951 & for the first time students of Orissa were freed from the administrative control of Patna University, as earlier it was administered from Bihar. Manorma & Utkalprava, Mayurbhanj chronicle, Bhanja-Pradip were few cultural-linguo journals published, promoted by Bhanja rulers which had featured almost all the literary doyens of that times and are considered today as rich treasure of culture, language & heritage. The ingredients of culture & rich heritageness was so deeply embedded that this soil later on produced many films-actors, producers, singers, directors, cinematographer and also provides panoramic view for film shooting till eighties. After this, the divisive politics has engulfed this region & its rich cultural heritage is stated to be encroached, crushed to the debris of shortlived consumerism .But as historians say- its cultural dimension is so vast that, time & trends may pass on it but unable to crush this century old Mahabharatian-Matsyadesa region-Mayurbhanj into dust. It's sublime heritageness is eluding the minds of future generations to witness.

Mahabharatian Heritage : Kichakeswari Temple

The many sites dating back to Mahabharatian era as the local myths & tales depict the site and events, Raja Kichaka, the brother–in-law of famous Viraat-Raja of Mahabharata fame had his capital at Khijingkota, as known to historians and today it is famous as Khiching and its presiding deity called Kichakeswari. It was believed that Kichakeswari was the presiding deity of Bhanja kings and in a number of places the idols of Maa Kichakeswari was found. In the Mayurbhanj palace itself, the western gate of the palace was the entry point of Maa Kichakeswari and it was closely worshipped by Bhanja kings exclusively by them only and outsiders were not allowed inside the temple. It is said that the temple Goddess was very effective (pratakhya)to the prayers of kings who inturn worship Her everyday and on some special occasions like, leading the armed forces on victory mission. The temple during the occasion of dussehra had witnessed large number of animal sacrifice including buffalo in its precincts which the royalty was fond of, to appease the deity. This palace temple was first opened to general public by Maharaja Pratap Chandra BhanjDeo during late 60's.Thereafter it was opened for all the time. The morning & evening worship bell of the temple reverberetes the whole palace precincts which several students used to witnessed as the palace was turned into a college by the Maharaja Purnachandra BhanjDeo. The temple has entry door like the Mughal era sculpture and its nata-mandap is like Hindu temple. The place where animals were sacrificed on tying on their heads has still withstood the time, engraving the blood of animal sacrifice, a saga of royalty.

The Kichakeswari Devi is the presiding deity of Bhanja kings till date and after the merger of Mayurbhanj state in 1949,its precincts was gradually diminished of celebrations like nitipuja, animal sacrifice etc for a longtime for dire want of funds and absence of royal patronage. But the present Maharaja Praveen Chandra BhanjDeo took a special interest in bringing back its past glory and accordingly reconstruction work begun and it has restored to its former glory. Now it performs its nitipuja and is open for public all the time. A number of photographs of this unique Mahabharatian era temple.

Jajneswara Mahadev Temple

The Maharaja Shri Ramchandra BhanjDeo had donated vast acres of land to his mentor & guru, the noted Sanskrit scholar Sri Gobinda Chandra Mohapatra who took the reins of administration while tutoring the adolescent Maharaja. In conform to guru-dakshina the Maharaja gave away lands on which Sri Mohapatra, the eminent author of translating Mahabharat in Sanskrit which later got sahitya akademi award had constructed a Shiva temple known as Jajneswar Temple in early 1900s. His own mortal body was engulfed to flame in this temple precincts. After the demise of Pandit Mohapatra his ancestors form a trust to look after this temple which was then outskirts of the town area, but with changing times it is now in the midst of crowded area. Later on the trustees have adjoined a Maa Durga temple to this main Shiva temple. Few photo documents to enliven the importance of this temple.

Benu Madhab Math : Paandava's place of worship

The study of Mahabharatian era Matsyadesa with greater depths and connected the rich, resplendent region of nature from many historians, researchers of past who has some or other way worked in this region, on subjects other than this. The famous such persons were Nilamani Senapati, S.N. Sarkar, J.K. Sahu, Dr K.C. Panigrahi, Dr H.K. Mahatab, Janmejay Sahu, P.K. Dash to name a few who have depicted the place & region in their writings as a natures gift to world, but many have unable to draw such similarities of Mahabharatian era relics, except in an sporadic manner. As stated earlier the area in Raruan where Sahadeva & Nakula were looking after the cow-cattles of Raja Biraaat is a fertile land where crops grow immensely and the people were fond of eking out their living out of cattle rearing & grazing. Apart from a little distance of Biraat fort in Khiching comes the natures paradise, Similipal sanctuary. The Panch Paandavas were stated to be accompanying Raja Biraat during his 'mrigayaa' or hunting spree to this region. The Pandava's along with Sairindri or Draupadi were also accompanying Raja Biraat & his queen Sudeshna during their hunting and legend established that there is a BeniMadhb math-temple in this deep, dense forest zone and which probably they were worshipping. Because under what circumstances a Krishna or BeniMadhab temple was constructed by whom, & when is still an enigma. As the Paandavas were the sakha's and the worshipper of Lord Krishna, they have devoted their stay in worshipping HIM in this thick forest secretly. The area now is under reserve forest division of Similipal Authority. The Fellow also consulted with some elders about this and they had also substantiated this view that, when there is no population movement nor it falls on the usual human habitat route this might have built by the Paandavas. The Fellow covered few other Bhanja heritage sites with greater depth.

Surya Nivas-Modern Management Institute

This heritage building was built since the days of Maharaja Pratap Chandra BhanjDeo and popularly known as Surya Nivas- or Sun House. The name does not indicate any special significance except that it is situated just few yards from famous Brahmo temple. Maharaja Sri Ramchandra BhanjDeo was an astute believers of Brahmo doctrines since the days of his schooling at Darjeeling & even fallen in love with famous Brahmo leader Keshab Chandra Sen's daughter. It was a different saga that this love couldn't materialize into marriage and the Maharaja setup Brahmo temple and there after Surya Nivas. The history of this heritage building states that, it was used for royal purpose and after the merger it has housed the Samabaya Parichalana Pratisthana or the Cooperative Management Institute to impart knowledge to strengthen the ongoing cooperative activities of the Govt. in this region. Therafter during 80's the then district administration has setup a Competitive & Career Training Centre behind its backyard rooms which continued so long the patronizer-officers were present in this area. But once they left the area, the training center was caught between groupism and affairs went into such a pass that the center was closed forever. However a local career orgn. JSP once proceeded with govt. to reopen this center but the elected representatives became a bar in its re opening .It was now clear that the elected representatives were not in favour of seeing the area's youth to be more & better qualified or successful in various competitive examinations as all the efforts were silenced. Now Surya Nivas only houses the cooperative management center in its front portion of heritage building and many years of neglect has threatened its ancient walls, floorings etc. The Fellow took few photographs of this heritage building.

HighCourt-Mayurbhanj

The benevolent Bhanja rulers knew that, their subjects were specially tribals & other economically poor who could not afford to move Highcourt then situated at Patna for justice. During 1947-57 the state comes under the jurisdiction of Patna High court & later on to Odisha Highcourt situated at Cattak. But the Maharaja's of Mayurbhanj fully realized the cost effectiveness in proceeding to higher courts, have setup a Highcourt in Mayurbhanj itself, during the royalty of Maharaja Sir Pratap Chandra BhanjDeo. Maharaja's such efforts were very much advanced of his times, maintains many historians. But after merger the govt. of Odisha ask the Maharaja to wihdraw this Highcourt as it merged under Odisha state & would have the same Highcourt jurisdiction of the state and cannot have another Highcourt. The Maharaja was agreed but urged the govt. to consider for setting a circuit bench of Odisha Highcourt in any future date, as his subjects were very much poor. Sixtyone years after also this merger provision was not acted on by the successive govt.'s in odisha which has resulted in regular strikes, bandhs on the demand of setting up a circuit court bench of Highcourt. Today the Mayurbhanj Highcourt building was used as the District Judges court. This heritage building has structures resembled with London's Buckingham Palace. Infact, the Maharaja's of Mayurbhanj were regular visitors to British royalty & had been greatly influenced by their style, domes and designs which reflected in several heritage buildings constructed by them.

Durbar Administrtion : Mayurbhanj State Bank

The Bhanja's were much advanced and ahead of their times in terms of ideas and building Institutions. They have built Mayurbhanj State Bank during the time of Maharaja Sir Pratap Chndra BhanjDeo which used as a royal-public treasury of funds. Interestingly many Maharja's like Bikaner, Saurashtra, Mysore, Hyderabad have setup their own State Banks, so also the Maharaja of Mayurbhanj. After independence ,the names of State Bank of Mysore, Bikaner, Rajasthan was remained intact ,but the gullible administrator have cleansed the word of Mayurbhanj in their bank and today it is simply known as State Bank of India. This ancient royal state bank is today used as a part of the local administration & revenue office works from this place. The entire Durbar admahistration has become completely taken over by the govt. of odisha and now collector-Dist. Magistrate sits in this durbar administration hall. But the grandeur marble statue of Maharja Sri Ramchandra BhanjDeo was unveiled years back as a tribute to his special benevolence which was garlanded every year on Dec.17, his anniversary day. The atmosphere of this heritage building is equivalent with the British royalty. Its sculptures, paintings and stairs all have reminded the once vast saga of royalty in this corridor of power. A bygone era splendour coupled with mystic royalty silence greets every visitor, whosoever crosses its corridors. The Fellow undertook a photo journey on this heritage building complex.

Localself Governance-Municipality Baripada

Maharaja Sri Ramchandra BhanjDeo inorder to provide his subjects good local administration has setup the Baripada Municipality in 1905 in this heritage royalty building which completes its centenary in 2005. It was beyond the thought of his time as many of his contemporary Maharaja's, rulers were even not organized their central administration or rules; the Maharaja's of Mayurbhanj could visualize the concept of local self govt. to better the civic life. Sanitation, road, streetlighting, burning ghats etc were the main activities of this municipality then, which today has expanded with the passage of time. Utkalmani Gopabandhu Dash, the noted freedom fighter, doyen, literature was once the Vice-chairperson of this municipality and served under Bhanja kings once, which was greatly benefited from his wisdom. This ancient heritage royal building was additioned with a new building during 2005; but the grandeur, aestheticness of the Paura-Parishad building & its inner council halls are a matter of visual treat which is situated just infront of Durbar administration complex or in today's official area. The former Durbar Administration Hall is used now as Collector's office and few views were taken to chronicle the glory, the grandeur of this heritage buildings established by Bhanja's.

Maa Jwalamukhi Mandir

Jwalamukhi considered as a royal deity exclusively here and a temple in the serene atmosphere of lake was built by Lalsaheb Pramod Chandra BhanjDeo, the younger brother of Maharaja which The Goddes today exclusively maintained & manged by Lalsaheb's family. This heritage temple goddess is in pure gold and its temple top is also covered with gold. The royal family members exclusively worship the deity and common public are allowed entry at specific time of the day and not always. The Lalsaheb's also promote a film production company in this name of Maa Jwalamukhi Films. The scholar-Fellow continue his study to several other historical places associated or believed to be habitated by Paandavas whose detail glimpse shall be provided in next report. The Fellow expresses his sincere gratitude for this unique scholarly study ever taken by anyone in this region through your kind Support.

Benisagar – The Mythical Place of Paanchali

The mythical place during Mahabharatian era-matsyadesa-Benisagar is a place to exude serenity & holiness in its environment.The place was very much a part of Mayurbhanj – then Matsyadesa until its merger in 1949 when some of its major regions were curved out to merge in odisha & few important places like Raibania, Olmara, Chinchda, Fenko including this Benisagar merged with Bihar & lateron in Jharkhand. A journey of five minutes from Mayurbhanj's Raruan block, one comes across through the signpost –Majhgaon block in West Singhbhum district in Jharkhand. A five minutes journey can take one to this most holiest places since Mahabharatian era. Benisagar as the name signifies a big pond, reservoir or lake even compared to a small dam situated amidst deep forest, cool breeze and out of noise pollution even that of a village. It was believed & ascertained by few historians that Paanchali during Paandava's agayatabasa' here was the royal accomplice of queen Sudeshna, of Raja Biraat and especially this place was used for bathing purpose of royalty. The queen along with her group of beauty maidens & Paanchali used to took bath in this water reservoir, away from commonmen's sight.It was once during her bath that Draupadi lost her 'beni"(hair) in this lake hence this name-Benisagar. The lake situated in a sylvan surroundings even today, quite away from public gaze. The entire area is covered with tall Sal trees, the hallmark of Mayurbhanj forests,where one could find a big dam like facilities have been erected. Just infront of this water pond one found the excavations of a big fort is in the process since last three years.The excavated materials include stonewares, idols builtup of black-mugni stones akin to the stone crafts of khiching. A number of Shivalingas are also found in this excavations for which it led to believe that, perhaps after secretely taking bath, the queensfolk used to worship Shiva in this temple.The excavations is in progress presently by ASI,Ranchi circle and a number of idols have been recovered in this region. But sadly the area once habitated in Mayurbhanj is now in Jharkhand. The Fellow – asked about it and got the reply that,it was very much a part of Jharkhand.Hence the forthcoming generations might never believe that it was once a part of matsyadesa –due to this political & administrative divisions, leading towards cultural bifurcation.A big museum of ASI is also under construction process and house all those excavated rare ancient materials, recovered during these digging.The quality of bricks used in these excavated fort-temple is similar to that of Haripur & Khiching –rectangular in shape but thickness is less than todays bricks.The scholar-fellow took few snaps of this place ideal for meditation as tranquility rules here but was prevented by the ASI staffs, not to photographed as it is in progress.However three photographs was already taken which are given herewith.

Keshna – Abode of Krishna'

Draupadi whose other name is Krishna was assigned this village situated just four km.from famous khiching temple after one crosses Ghikhali village on the roadside.Both the side of road one could witness a number of stoneware artisans are busy in ripping the black mugni stones and out of it, they used to design various eyecatching stonecrafts-idols of different kinds, animals other household uscable items are being forked out from these stones. Around 200 craftsman lives in this area alone of which 300 are households. Almost all the major adults are being trained to become a craftsman of stone artistry, but with days passed however their number started receding as new generes are opting jobs outside this traditional mode of earning. The villagers believed that their village keshna have a never ending supply of black-mugni stone out of which they used to earn their livelihood since generations. This black mugni stone is widely used in construction of famous khiching temple once. The villagers are proud of their crafts and is lamenting on the resource crunch in this stone arts & crafts.Few years ago a bank and a non-govt. orgn. has organized a workshop to build the capacities of stone crafts but greater efforts with funds to improve their skill, living is needed in this Mahabharatian site. Few photographs taken by the scholar of this area are given.

Biraat Sena- Mahabharatian relics

The existence of Biraat Sena in this Mahabharatian famous matsyadesa signifies that, Raja Biraat belongs to this region and interestingly a troupe called "Biraat sena" is in existence since long. They might have ascendants to the members of Biraat-sena(military) community. This sena this month staged a dharna in protest on the rising terror menace in the country and paid tribute to the deceased persons of Mumbai blast at Taj. The solidarity it expresses from far away a place from Mumbai speaks the greater consciousness of this sena. This sena is led by persons of Mahanta community. Mahanta's are neither tribals nor general- their physical features are sharp, tallsome of their habits are similar to local tribes & some are like general higher castes. They might have descendants of Biraat Raja's army, believes many,as a number of material evidence signifies that like their lifestyles, their taste for superior quality,their demand from exclusion from ST list before independence & now for reinclusion in this same list, their livelihood pattern mostly by cultivation, cow, cattle rearing & dependence on agriculture etc.

Sanskruti Bhavan & Chaitra Parva'

The much awaited Sanskruti-Bhavan (cultural center) of the district which was under costruction since last few years was inaugurated by hon'ble Chiefminister of the state, just a day before the famous chaitra-parva. The new cultural complex, a two-storied building grandeur official complex was built at a cost of around 65 lakh it is known from cultural deptt. sources and is situated just infront of the famous chaitra-parva ground or 'chhau-padia'. The cultural complex would synthesise the various aspects of rich cultural heritages of this region and it would of great use for researchers in coming days. The Fellow also engraphed an article compiling several aspects of famous chhau dance popularly known as chaitra-parva here where this folk dance tradition is still alive since the Bhanja kings in the minds of people in this region. A description writeup on this famous dance form was made by the Fellow in contribution to this cultural dance form in a seperate published form.

Simleswara-pitha of Similipal

Simleswara pitha in this famous Similipal region is another cultural heritage site of ancient years situated by Budhabalanga river in Golmundhakata grampanchayat under Bangiriposi block. The village Simla was surrounded with river & dense forest and legend has it that a black cow crossing the river came to this dense forest stood on a black stone without the knowledge of anyone. Once the cowherd boy Ram Behera followed this black cow and found that after crossing river Balanga it reached to a particular spot and stood there to pour milk on a black stone. The cowherd boy told this tale to his owner Fakir Giri which confirm that it is the miracle of Lord Shiva. Thereafter the simla villagers constructed a palm roof house over it and which was lateron developed into a temple by the local zamindar Minaketan Das in 1915 .The festivities of this Simleswara-pitha is spiritually uplifting under the scenic Similipal foothills.

Purnachandra Industrial Centre

This is one of the heritage building since the Bhanja kings have enriched the local region with their timeless contribution. Maharaja Purna chandra BhanjDeo the son of Sri Ramchandra Bhanj Deo was adolscent & reading at Mayo college, Ajmer at the time of the death of his father. The then British Court of wards Mr Philips & Mr Peck took the reins of Mayurbhanj state till 1920, he matures into kingship. Maharaja Purnachandra BhanjDeo was a benevolent ruler like his father and could be equal to Mughal king, Shahjehan for his lavish royalty & construction of timeless, palatial buildings which stand today as heritage site. Infact many buildings, forts of grandeur today witnessed to his contribution. Inorder to accelerate the technical progress, skill to be utilized for industrial purpose of the youths, he setup the one & only PCI popularly known as Purna Chandra Industrial Centre where students were provided free training by instructors in the areas of plumbing, stitching, knitting, embroidering. Maharani Takhatkumari undertook the entire cost for this complex which today stands as a symbol of rich cultural heritage site. Lateron after the merger of Mayurbhanj state, the state govt. took the reins of this technical training center and converted into exclusively for women in 1998. Thereafter many addition on the frontage of this heritage building like a stage-platform for cheap publicity by few has reduced its glory. Two view of this heritage structure is given.

Banabihari Mandir

Banabihari temple of Shri Krishna was dedicated by the Maharani Takhatkumari on the lake side at Takatpur. This heritage temple was remained neglected for years together till it was recovered from dilapidated condition on the initiatives of few youths which is gradually restored to its pristine glory. This dilapidated heritage temple site was covered by this Fellow on photographs, which todays under the management of debottar department.

Jhinjhir-bandh' Jubilee Park

The Bhanja kings Belgadia palace is surrounded with a natural lake popularly known as Jhinjhir-bandh meaning chain –lake which was stated to be the place of a deity. Lateron this lake was beautified with a park called Jubilee park and many a flower, fruit garden with sitting arrangements were erected to upgrade the lake into a beautiful tourist place.

According to another popular folklore, once a cowherd boy was guarding the cows and found one of its milchcow is not in the group. He made frantic search of this cow and found it in the bank of river Gangahaar where it was standing near a kakharu leaf tree and milk was pouring from its body. The next day he also found that this partcular cow is regularly going to that particular spot and sprinkling milk underneath this kakharu tree. He narrated this entire incident to villagers who came and digged the place and found Shiva linga, which later on led for establishments of today's famous Kakharua Baidyanath Pitha. A nuimber of villagers had donated each three maan (around a bigha) of land for this pitha for which this area is known as Manatri meaning three- mana and lateron Bhanja Kings were instrumental for constructing this heritage site structure.

This heritage-cultural temple was probably built during later 14th & early 15th century AD according to few other scholar- historians, when the famous Puri Gajapati Raja Kakharua Dev and in Mayurbhanj Maharaja Balabhadra BhanjDeo was ruling this region. During the visit of Puri-Gajapati the construction of this temple might have begun. Another mythology holds that during 1556 AD it was built by Mahaaja Baidyanath BhanjDeo who was also the builder of famous Shri Hari Baladev jew(Jaganath) temple in Baripada. The fact is historically verifiable as the structures, domes, natamandir of Kakharua pitha are largely identical with this Jagannath temple and it is quite different from usual shiva temples. He established the idols of Lord Jagannath in this pitha hence an ideal place of worship for Hari (Vishnu) & Hara (Shiva). Everyday the temple includes a kakharu as its prasaad and despite a shiva-pitha it usually observes all the festivals of Jagannath temple with equal fervour & grandeur like ratha-yatra, devasnan, jhulan, dolapurnima. But the most important & unique festival here is Maha Shivaratri which usually observed for a fortnight every year with lakhs of devotees thronging from allover. This rich heritage site & temple have hundreds of acres of land engaged by Bhanja rulers for the smooth management of deity & temple with grandeur. Baba Kakharua Baidyanath is surrounded with Shri Loknath, Shri Maliknath, Shri Kundanath, Shri Barahnath, Shri Swapneswarnath apart from Mahveer-Hanuman, Maa Durga.

The Fellow-scholar covers this rich cultural zone to capture the gaiety of heritageness with its raw flavour during Maha Shivaratri and the most scenic part is the appearance of deity from the river bed. A number of photo-essays with a published report in Oriya on this site is given herewith exclusively to depict the unique heritageness of this place.

Mahabharatian interaction

The number of heritage structures, monuments despite scorching heat wave and put an attempt to bring back the ancient memory of this Matsyadesa of Mahabharat fame, presently named as Mayurbhanj. The Fellow had interacted with two scholars in this regard and brought the ambience of Mahabharat fame matsyadesa which is symmetrically manifesting on observance of folklore, physical structures along with repleting memory of localities. The biggest discovery is: there is an area known as Paanch-pidh which is locally known as 'village for five' which have villages/areas in the names of Paanch-pandavas of Mahabharat fame. These are Arjuna-pidh or village-Arjuna Judhistir-pidh, Bhim-pidh etc which many believes that, perhaps habitated by the Paandavs during their agyaat - basa to this region, far away from Hastinapur. However no scholars or researchers of repute have worked upon this idea so far which is gaining strengthen with evidences of Paandavas- agyaatbasa period in this matsyadesa - Mayurbhanj.

Purnachandra Mandir

This famous heritage monuments was built by Maharani Takhatkumari , the wife of Maharaja Purnachandra Bhanj Deo whose premature death put the maharani into sorrow and she built a structure in the name of her late husband to commemorate their loving memory. This structure is known as Purnachandra Mandir, is situated amidst sprawling 3 acres of garden near the Maharaja's court office chamber which today housed district Magistrate office. This heritage building was built during 1928 and every year on 7 April, the demise day of late Maharaja was observed with pomp & ceremony by giving alms to poor & food to hungry by the descendants of Maharajas. The garden aross this structures is decorated with number of rare variety of flowers, plants, trees and is managed by the royalty till this day. Inside it, the statue of Maharaja

Purachandra BhanjDeo is worshipped.

Baripada Club

This ancient heritage building was constructed by the royalty during 50's which was used by royals, british-sahebs & other important dignitaries which was later on managed by common men with changing times and presently high officials, other dignitaries used it. This heritage structure has since long providing a major cultural hub for many in this city of royalty.

Banthia-Jaganath Mandir

Apart from Shri Shri HariBaladev jew-Jaganath temple built by Maharaja Baidyaath Bhanj Deo in 1575, there is another unique temple of Lord Jaganath popularly known as San-Jaganath or Banthia-Jaganath. The idols of Jaganath, Balavadra, Suvadra are usually very small, approximately half of the length of the usual Jaganath idols. The temple was built by Maharaja Srinath Bhanj Deo during 1863-1867 AD. This ancient temple follows all the rituals of Jaganath temple and is situated in today's center of the town. Its adjacent areas have been encroached & constructed by many as a result this ancient temple have shrinked never before. The most interesting feature is: its rathyatra. A small chariot (rath) is erected which is usually pulled by children below 14 years every year. This Banthia (small) Jaganath have everything come in small sizes starting from its idol to chariot. Its mausibadi, the place where Lord Jaganath, Balavadra, Suvadra rests for nine days is being observed at nearby Sanskrit −tol -college which was also built during this period. Though a little bit restoration work of this heritage structures made some years back, the gradual encroachments from all its side and the administrative inability to remain vacant this heritage zone has gradually diminishing the historicity of this temple.

Christian Cemetry

The royalty of Mayurbhanj was kind hearted & each ruler has displayed his passion for secularism long before secularism has engraved in the Indian constitution. This has tremendously boosted the images of Bhanja Rulers. Their policy with all - be it muslims, Christians, Hindus, Sikhs or Santhal- was same; welfare of all. Even Maharajas like Sri Ramcandra BhanjDeo had patronized Christians in many ways for which a number of Christian hamlets, institutions, organizations grew up over these years. Lands, funds and royal patronage were extended to Christian minority community to grew up as a special religion. This royal patronage gave them immense morale to develop a strong Christian base here unlike any other areas in the state. Maharaja Sri Ramchandra BhanjDeo has given land for construction of churches, cemetry in 1902 by a royal-sanand (royal-order) on which a number of churches and the lone Cemetry was constructed. The Cemetry today found enroute national highway –5 and exists just at the Murgabadi circle. This cemetry have housed several Christian preachers, functionaries who came here to preach new things and is a rest house amidst serene surroundings till today. The area was earlier peaceful but today its main door is also encroached for the use of a local fish, meat bazaar. Its southern side is covered by an upcoming nursing home by few as a result the glory, the ambience it was earlier exuding have greatly diminishing with each passing day. Chances are, if this heritage site is not protected with strong measures, than soon this cemetery of a community would lost to builders, encroachers.

Nrutya-kothi of Bhanja's

The journey in this Mahabharat fame Matsyadesa with encounters to a number of issues affecting the cultural heritage institutions with the onslaught of time. The Bhanja rulers were patrons of aesthetics, art & culture. A palace- heritage building was devoted by Bhanja rulers for promotion of classical & other forms of dance. This two storied heritage building was famous in the name of nrutya-kothi or dance palace during royalty. It was learnt that a number of well known dancers from all over the country used to perform their dancing skill and highly rewarded by Bhanja rulers. Built during the time of Maharaja Sri Ram Chandra Bhanj Deo this heritage building was remained neglected for years together and is encroached & surrounded by some illegal dhabawallas who have opened hotels in front of this heritage building .Even few timber mafias have turned this heritage palace for keeping their illegally cut timbers from local forest as no inspecting officer could ever search this heritage building premises. Lateron this palace was taken by govt. and the district food, supply department functions from this palace. But the palace has developed cracks & unsuitable for habitation and was left by officials. In 2005 this heritage palace was razed to the ground and the govt.has undertaken construction for a four storied building to put the district treasury here. Hence yesterdays nrutya-kothi is fast transforming into today's district treasury.

Karam parva – A Cultural Fiesta

The local tribes as well as mahanta, kurmi, bhumij, teli, gauda, kumbhar, khandayat communities have a cultural jamboree called karam-parva Ekadasi. After the cessation of rain months the onset of winter this celebration was being observed with pomp & gaiety. This heritage cultural trends was also observed during the Bhanja's in the Mayurbhanj palace itself, the elders say. Unmarried girls were putting black & green grams,kolatha- a local pulse grown here in a bamboo base locally known as dala'. After putting all these pulses two days before the celabration it generates sprouts on which the leaves & branches of karam tree were planted known as 'Jawa' which is being worshipped by all .During worship the songs they used to sang were in the language of malwa- used by mahanta community. In a village several household put two branches of karam leaves tree and worship it on fasting to fulfill their heartfelt desires .The karam devata is believed to be a brahmin Raja once upon a time and his symbol is keli-kadamba tree- a locally grown plant ,who had lost everything -wealth,   power,   position &   become directionless and even used to stay in a village as a farmer. Since then to commemorate his ordeals, his subjects were believed to be observing karamparva. The typical village flavour dominates the entire karam puja day whose sentiment dates back to centuries, said a number of village elders.A published article is given by the fellow on this typical cultural fiesta.

Kurmi's Cultural demand

The kurmi-mahanta community have agitated over their inclusion again into ST fold. Their culture were of like a tribal community and long back they had demanded to declare them into general category but of late they have started realizing that re-inclusion into ST fold would give them better advantage & hence agitations in the forms of meeting ,community mobilisation is found to be raising its ugly head. Some call it politics but some view it as a social malady but such a twist have given a new turn to their cultural affinity in this Mahabharatian-matsyadesa region again.

Maa Hingula-Pitha Temple

The fellow covered a number of Heritage institutions to document the glory of Mahabharatian era -Matsyadesa in this region. The road en -route to Badsahi-khunta comes a big jungle where the famous Maa Hingula temple is situated and considered a very powerful deity by many in this region. She provides all fulfillment whosoever wishes anything at her feet. Mata was 'appeared' under a peppal tree where the villagers had erected a temple. It grew into become an institution with active support of devotees making it a fund of around Rs 80 lakh. . In 2006 there was dispute over the two groups of sevayats who claims the huge fund for themselves. It led into legal battles and the local administration to interfere in the matter and last year the court gave a ruling in favour of one group who took away all the funds and even shifted the entire deity to few kilometers away from this main pitha. However few other devotees again worship her under the same tree where she appeared first and within a year there is again rush for devotees in this place. The worship is done in a very systamatic manner, first near the jajna-kunda the devotee is put on a 'sankalpa' and thereafter puja is being performed in the main temple. In a specific date of each year, Maa Hingula-yatra is performed where everything pours into a big fire pond and it was celebrated by lakhs of devotees in this region. There is also a wish-fulfilling tree behind the temple where devotees ties spade to fulfill their wishes and Maa Hingula is believed to be most powerful in fulfilling her devotees wishes and it is one of the reason that lakhs throngs to this sacred place even if it is situated deep inside the forest.

NH Inspection Bunglow

The Bhanja rulers were instrumental in building numbers of royal establishments with grandeur which withstood all the tribulations of time. This NH- IB or todays national-highway inspection bunglow was built by Maharaja Sri Ramchandra Bhanj Deo where the British sahebs like Andrew Fraser was staying to supervise the railway work before 1905. The sahebs after construction of railway here left and the same building was converted an inspection bunglow by govt. Its British era construction style and simple texture give it a look of a saheb-bunglow which still able to maintain its heritageness.

Circuit House

The Bhanja rulers were adopter of modernity, way ahead of their times and in this regard the exposure of Sri Ramchandra Bhanj Deo with western cultures, visit & interaction with Britishers all led the Maharaja to construct a lavish building during 1935-37 which is known as Circuit House or Bishram Bhavan. It is since then used as a rest house for visiting dignatories to this region like ministers, governors, high officials coming from state govt. or Centre . They used to take rest after a day long circuitory-official visits in this area. This heritage building is one of the most lavish building which has also upgraded by the successive govt's to suit to the changing needs of the time. This heritage building has enough space for keeping numbers of vehicles as well as several suites to accommodate a number of visiting dignitories to this area. In 2005 a major addition was made by district collector, V

K Pandiyan when he built a mansion behind this heritage bunglow to accommodate more numbers of visiting dignitories simultaneously. This has added new dimension to this heritage bunglow.

Railways : Narrow – Broad gauge

As stated earlier the Maharaja was keen that his subjects should avail journey facilities at a lesser price and railway was best option. The historical Rupsa-Talbandh railway track in narrow-gauge is a rare historical monuments like the Darjeeling railways. In 1905 this train line was opened and linked at Rupsa which connects with major railways of the country. After the demise of Bhanja rulers this narrow-gauge train was cut short between Rupsa-Bangriposi and again between Rupsa-Baripada for a long. Many of its historic viewed tracks especially between Bangriposi to Talbandh inside the famous Similipal sanctuary was a rare feat which is no more today. Its historic tracks are also gradually disappeared and it took 100 yeas - in 2005-06 to convert this railway from narrow to broad gauge by the present govt after years of demand. Its halting station like krishnachandrapur, Betnoti, Jugal, Jugpura, Thakurtota amidst sylvan surroundings, all were built by Bhanja rulers which has now upgraded and a train between state capital Bhubaneswar - Baripada is running presently. But the historic train & its stations are still a rare monuments to watch by many visitors.

Baptist Church

The Bhanjas were secular as they allow all religion to flourish simultaneously whose evidence is popularization of Christianity. Apart from famous KCPur church both the Catholic & Protestant groups were promoted by Maharaja's and on their given land, both the sects had developed their respective churches. This Baptist church built during 1928 is situated in front of the Maharaja's Durbar – todays court office. This church was become the abode of many missionaries like Graham Staines who with their dedicated works had flourish the glory of this ancient institution. After his brutal killing in 1999, the church management has erected a hospital in memory of Staines where services to poor & leapers have taken up as a mission . Every Sunday here Christians assembled to Pray God.

Maa Santoshi Temple

In last one decade the tremendous devotion & fulfillment of wishes of several led to construct this Maa Santoshi temple which grew up from a heap of stone into glittering idols where thousands visits daily to worship her and more especially on Friday where women keep solah-sukravaar-vrata for their wish fulfillment and as a matter of focused devotion. The Maa Santoshi temple was grew up on the sole contributions of many devotees- again an established proof of peoples beliefs and faith in a higher power. Similar another temple is : Tarini temple on the road to Banthia-Jaganath temple where thousands gathered especially on Tuesday and it become an abode of power center.

Development : committed or political !

The Mahabharat fame Matsyadesa –Mayurbhanj this month again witnessed a number of violence with several bandhs for politicizing the issue of cessation of Mayurbhanj by tribal political outfits – Jharkhand Morchas. It has snowballed the agitation for reiterating its demand for taking this district along with two other-Keonjhar, Sundergarh – all forests, mineral rich to adjacent

Jharkhand state for a greater Jharkhand. The intellectuals to commonmen, all have agitated and several bandhs was organized demanding boycott of jharkhandi leaders. The Fellow-scholar also came with informative published reports which opens the pandoras box. It says presently all the three tier govt.-from Panchayat to Parliament are in the control of Jharkhandi leaers since last 20 years directly and the amount of pilferage of development funds by them is unimaginable.Their tendency to grab more with blackmail politics has become the biggest hurdles for Mayurbhanj's development. The Fellow also gave a roadmap for Mayurbhanj's development by publishing a researched articles that – mere slogan is not enough,what is needed is strong commitment for development of this region.The Sal leaves- khali,dona;the Sabai grass – from rope to other items-units which are operational allover and eighty percent tribals of this region eke out their living out of it needed to be strengthened,as no organized effort was ever made by anyone,or whatever was made is inadequate. The number of closed indutrial units like Paper board unit at Dantiamuhan, the sugarcane factory at Jharpokharia, the powerloom of Takatpur and many more sick units needed to be revived. The state Bamboo Board need to invest in the huge bamboo sector,so as to tame the resing unemployment ration & growing social disturbances. The research findings were first of its kind & unique and also gave a roadmap to development of Mahabharat fame Matsyadesa –Mayurbhanj district.

Merger-Division of Mayurbhanj

This month witnessed a major spurt in violence on the cessionist demand of Jharkhand party for division of Mayurbhanj district adjacent to Jharkhand state. The demand of bifurcation of Mayurbhanj state was stiffly opposed by people allover against the jharkhandis who took the govt. to ransom for giving support during the vote of confidence held in this month. It has a greater significance with regard to the cultural identity of this region apart from its political milieu. Mayurbhanj, the old Matsyadesa where paandavas spent one year during their agayaatbasa has a rich cultural history which was in its zenith during the Bhanja Kings. In 1935-36 Mayurbhanj state was the first royalty to initiate the process of democracy with the involvement of people which led the way to its partial bifurcation at the time of merger. As areas like Sareikela, Kharswan, Chakulia, Fenko, Bankura, Dhalbhumgarh, Olmara were bifurcated from its royal map to adjacent Bihar-Jharkhand-Bengal-Odisha areas. Since then the odia people living in these belts are undergoing with an identity conflict as they were subjected to the influence of an alien culture or a mixed one of Bengali-odia-Bihari influences simultaneously. This has created a wide gap in these Mayurbhanjities who were once subject of princely state .In 1999, the demand of Jharkhand state was curved out from Bihar and people thought the Jharkhand politics have been subsided. But the cheap way of popularity by few political leaders has put flame on the fire as they have reiterated for making a greater Jharkhand by again curving out Mayurbhanj and two other districts from Odisha. The people came out to street to oppose such divisive demands as it would create more cultural conflicts in the persons residing in this region. This even led to violent demonstration & proves that further cultural divisions in lines of cheap politics by few would endangered the region's distinct cultural identities of these people. The tribal culture amalgamated with ethnic history and a rich heritage has so far able to retain the distinct identity of societies here which would crack to ground, if further politicalised bifurcation would come to replay. It again echoed the distinct cultural identity of Mayurbhanj.

Bhanja Rulers: The Builder of Modern Mayurbhanj

The Bhanja rulers are the builders of modern Mayurbhanj, like Akbar was for the Mughals. However the North Odisha University has a prime responsibility to introduce a course curriculum on Mayurbhanj History, its ruling dynasties -the Bhanja rulers who had started their reign since 612 AD from Adi Singh to Pradeep Chandra BhanjDeo. Their benevolent contribution has immensely contributed the social, economic & other developments in an era when many kingdoms were grappled with injustice, poverty & penury. The history of Mayurbhanj or Bhanja Rulers were not only the times & life of royalty but it would also be a parallel journey into the history of other trends,persons like socio-economic-cultural ,scholarly pursuits - art,literature and also persons like Gopal Praharaj-the author of Purnachandra odiya Bhashakosh ; Gopabandhu Dash-the doyen of Satyabadi & also the states the then vice-chairman ;Fakirmohan Senapati-the vysakabi ,Utkal gaurav Madhusudan Das,Radhanath Ray,Gobinda Chandra Mohapatra-author of translated Mahabharat,Harekrishna Mahatab-the strongman of odisha who had played a pivotal role in Mayurbhanj's history & many others who were patronized & promoted by Bhanja kings.

Art, culture, painting,s culpture, governance, judiciary, banking, railway, educational developments, livelihood generation in every sector & sphere,Mayurbhanj and its rulers played a very significant role. They were modern to the sense that, they allowed an Airplane landing zone during IInd world war, formed a Cooperative with the British cooperative father Sir Daniel Hamilton,construct Baldiha, Haldia, Badjore dams,even generated electricity from the flowing streams of Similipal sanctuary which are very modern concepts & way ahead of their times and the Bhanja Rulers with their outlook could dreamt and acted on it. For their such advancement of ideas & its implementation, they deserve specific recognition in this Mayurbhanj History course-curriculum like the Delhi & many other Universities since its beginning has implemented special couses on the history of Mughals & other Sultans, Laxmibai, Malviya as a special study package & part of their tribute to those rulers ,great minds on whose soil,contribution it stands today.

A group of Scholars need to be evolved to study their contributions in the overall development allover Odisha, India which is not only confined to Mayurbhanj alone. Starting from their funding support to Benaras Hindu University (BHU)under the invitation of Sri Madan Mohan Malviya to Utkal University where Sir Pratap Chandra BhanjDeo was the first Chancellor ;for Bhanja rulers unique contributions to the educational development allover the state to settingup of a Chair ; from Sri Ramchandra BhanjDeo Medical college to promotion of Mayurbhanj Chhau about which this generation & coming also is completely unaware and ask very often : who are Bhanja Rulers - what is their contributions ?

The NOU-North Odisha University today stands as their first contributions, as dating back to 1924 the Maharani

Takat Kumari has donated around 267 acres of land for the proposed university. Does it not unobligatory on our part if this university wouldnot incorporate a special study-course-curriculum on them ? The beginning of a course on Bhanja Rulers of Mayurbhanj would also need the task for marathon research, documentation to compile the unorganized datas in this proposed department of Mayurbhanj History. It is time that the intelligent leaders of the state must put all their effort to start this new department & course as a major tribute to Bhanja kings, kingdoms before the new generation would ask – who is Pratap Chandra Bhanj !!!

MANAGEMENT OF HERITAGE ART CULTURAL INSTITUTIONS

BHANJA- VIGNETTE IN MAHABHARAT FAME MATSYADESA - MAYURBHANJ

Bhanja's were ruler par-excellence as they believed in peoples overall development. Originally migrated from Jaipur, Rajsthan-Bhanja's laid down the dynasty of ruling in the year 598 AD onwards whose saga continues till the merger of Mayurbhanj state in January 1, 1949. A peep into the chronology of Bhanja kings ruled in Mayurbhanj state-believed to be the Mahabharat fame Matsyadesa.

Order   of

Succession

From – To: A D

----

1.   Maharaja   Jai
Singh
598 – 618

2. Deo 618 – 656	Adi	Bhanj
3. Deo 656 – 689	Nilambar	Bhanj
4. BhanjDeo 689 - 726		Laxmanagraj
5. BhanjDeo 726 – 764		Biseswara
6. BhanjDeo 764- 804		Bharat
7. BhanjDco 804 -839		Dillipeswar
8. BhanjDeo 839 – 878		Bamdev
9. BhanjDeo 878 – 916		Basudev
10. BhanjDeo 916 – 960		Keshari
11. BhanjDeo 960 – 996		Narayan
12. BhanjDeo		Nilakantha

996 – 1028

13. BhanjDeo   Birkeshwari

1028 – 1064

14. Bhanjdeo   Kapileswar

1064 – 1100

15. BhanjDeo   Trilochan

   1100-1138

16. BhanjDeo   Dasrathi

      1138 – 1164

17. BhanjDeo   SriKrishna

   1164 – 1195

18. BhanjDeo   Gadadhar

   1195 – 1238

19. BhanjDeo   Arneswar

      1238 – 1264

20. BhanjDeo   Gopinath

      1264 – 1279

21. BhanjDeo   Radhakrishna

1279 – 1301

22. BhanjDeo   Prithwinath

1301 – 1334

23.   Baikunthanath

BhanjDeo
1334 – 1360

24.   Bireswara
BhanjDeo
  1360 – 1390

25.   Ramchandra
BhanjDeo
1390 – 1423

26.   Balabhadra
BhanjDeo
1423 – 1464

27.   Harikrushna
BhanjDeo
1464 – 1491

28.   Nilakantha
BhanjDeo
1491 – 1520

29.   Santei
BhanjDeo
      1520 – 1556

30.   Baidyanth
BhanjDeo
  1556 – 1600

31.   Jagannath
BhanjDeo
  1600 – 1643

32.   Harihara
BhanjDeo
  1643 – 1688

33.   Sarbeswara
BhanjDeo
1688 – 1711

34.		BirBikramaditya
BhanjDeo		1711
– 1728		
35.		Raghunath
BhanjDeo		
1728 – 1750		
36.		Chakradhar
BhanjDeo		
1750 – 1761		
37.		Damodar
BhanjDeo		
1761 – 1796		
38.	Maharajeswari	Sumitradevi
BhanjDeo		1796 – 1810
39.	Maharajeswari	Jamunadevi
BhanjDeo		1810 – 1813
40.		Tribikram
BhanjDeo		
1813 – 1823		
41.		Jadunath
BhanjDeo		
1823 – 1863		
42.		Srinath
BhanjDeo		
1863 – 1868		
43.	Krushna	Chandra
BhanjDeo		1868 –
1882		
44.		SriRamchandra
BhanjDeo		
1882 – 1912		
45.		Purnachandra

BhanjDeo
1914 – 1922
46.   Pratapchandra
BhanjDeo
1923 – 1967
47.   Pradipchandra
BhanjDeo
1967 – 2005
48.   Pravinchandra
BhanjDeo
2005 –
SECTION : C
PHOTO ESSAYS
References & Bibilography

Mayurbhanj of My Times-Gobinda Chandra Mahapatra, 1896.
Mo Samayara Odisha, Dr K C Panigrahi
Matsyadesara dana-Sirish Parida
Chaitraparva journal-Mayurbhanj pratisthana
Bhanja pradip 1934-Mayurbhanj state press
Deokund diary-TOI
Charukla ra apurva samanaya, Khiching-Hemanta Kumar Dash
Karam Ekadasi-Nepal Mohanta
Sambad Uttaraodisha edition, Nov 2007
Archaeolgical mystery of Raibania-Rabindra Senapati
Sad story of a royal building-Eastern Times, J B Dash, Nov, 08
Discovery of Mahabharatian era civilization in Itagarh, Dubigarh-JB Dash, Prajatantra & Samaya saptahiki
Subterrain of Paandavas agayatabasa-Panchpidh-Sri

Krushna samal, Janabani

Ancient civilization unearthed-Indian Express, JB Dash, 1997

Pandavghera-sambad uttarodisha, 24 Jan 2010

Maa Ambika of Baripada/Vokta/Institutionalisation of Mayurbhanj chhau-JB Dash, Pratisthan journal,1998

Medias in Mayurbhanj-JB Dash, 2001

Swarnayuga pravartak Maharaja Sri Ramchandra Bhanj-Dr B.Lenka

Mayurbhanj state Gazetter-Nilamani senapati, 1957

The Author expresses his sincere gratitude to those number of brochures, book, reference journals, periodicals & scholars whose insights & support have enriched this wonderful Mahabharatian era journey in Matsyadesa-Mayurbhanj.

----- Author, Fellow.

HERITAGE MONUMENTS OF MATSYADESA-MAYURBHANJ AND BHANJA RULERS

Study & Documentation of the Heritage Buildings, Structures, Monuments, sites of

Mahabharat Era and Bhanja Rulers

JAANAKI BALLAV DASH

SeniorFellow, Culture

Govt.of India

CHAPTERS : SECTION -A

The Journey for Mahabharatian era sites:

Raibania Fort

Heriatege Air Fields
Jubilee Library
Lulung-Sitakund
Raghunathjew shrine
Bhudhara Chandi
Jhinkpada temple
Bhanja's-worshipper of Bishnu cult
Mayurbhanj Textiles
Naaagra-bhadi
Belgadia palace
Budharaula Mahadev
Mayurbhanj palace-a site of royal heritage
Makarsankranti mela
Talsari Tourism zone
Jajneswara Mahadev
Kakharua Baidyanath
Manatri & Kuradiha garh
Baruneswar Mahadev
Sanskriti Bhavan
Simleshwar pitha
Purnachandra Mandir
Baripada club
Banthia Jaganath Mandir
Christian cemetery
Maa Hingula pitha
NH Inspection bunglow
Circuit House
Railaways-Narrow & Broad gauge
Baptist Church
Maa Santoshi Temple
Bamanghati Garhi temple
Ma Kichakeswarigarh-Bahalda

Dandbose Air strip
MaharajaKrushnachandra Highschool
SuryaNivas
Highcourt-Mayurbhanj
Durbar Admn-Mayurbhanj state Bank
Localself Govt-Baripada Municipality
Maa Jwalamukhi Temple
Karamparva-cultural fiesta
Kurmis cultural demand
Deokund-A major shaktipitha
Kamardiha Matha-A ruinous site
Cremation place or personal holdings
Sarada Mandir
Saraskshetra of Lord Jaganath
Chahla Heritage resthouse
Astamprahari-badi-pala culture on wane
Merger-Division ofMayurbhanj
Development-committed or Political
Bhanja Rulers-The Builders of Mayurbhanj
Rulers chart in chronology
SECTION : C
Photo Essays

Mahabharatian Heritage-Samibrukhya
Heritage Kichakgada or Todays Khiching
Mahabharatian heritage-Historic Benisagar
Mahabharatian relics-Raibania Fort
Heritage Haripur Fort relics
Narrowgauge heritage Train
Jajneswar Mahadev
Purnachandra Industrial Centre
Circuit House-old & new

National highway heritage house
SantoshiMaa Mandir
Purnachandra Mandir
Maa Jwalamukhi Mandir
Mayurbhanj Durbar-Todays collectorate
Baruneswar Mahadev
Municipality's heritage house
Krushnachandra school
SuryaNivas-heritage house
Highcourt Mayurbhanj
Sanskruti Bhavan
Jubilee Park
Heritage Baripada club
Maa Sarada Mandir
Saraskshetra Jaganath
Nagrabhadi heritage building
Maa Kichakeswari Baripada Temple
Maingate of Belgadia palace
Sri Haribaladevjew temple
Heritage Mayurbhanj Palace
Mayurbhanj State Bank
Resthouse Nichuapada
Heritage Maharani Dharmasala
Maa Dwarsuni Mandir
Jhinkeswar Mahadev
Dalimbeswar Mahadev, Kainsari
Baptist church
Heritage Christian cemetery
Heritage Jubilee library
Kichakeswari-Bahalda
ASIs neglect-Itagarh, Dubigarh
Kakharua Baidyanath pitha

Deokund

Maharaja Sri Ramchandra Bhanj statue

Maa Hingula pitha

Seva sangha heritage building

Acknowledgement

The Fellow Author expresses his sincere gratitude with Thanks to all in the Ministry of Culture, Govt. of India for its kind & unconditional Support for this documentation work, without which it couldn't have been possible.

This documentation is dedicated with a hope that the future generation would come to terms with our aeon-old tradition, culture and the govt would make all these virgin spot-sites believed to be of Mahabharata era during Paandava's agayatabasa of a year to develop these as major, important heritage tourist sites on the roadmap provided here. It is an humble attempt to unearth the Matsyadesa in today's Mayurbhanj & all those aspects which signify these beliefs.

Senior Fellow

PREFACE

It is a lifetime opportunity to be a part of history-maker in contributing to strengthen those myths, pables which are in circulation since long, although in a distorted manner. Since my childhood, there were inebriated attempt by few to amplify the beliefs that – Mayurbhanj was the Matsyadesa of Mahabharata – and from this one sentence, starts the development of this intensive research study. The many myths, relics, heritage sites and special characteristics lend belief to this thought which has resulted in this monumental work, a maiden attempt to amplify those aspects, sites which form a distinct part of Paandava's sojourn.

Mahabharat-the great epic of yore describes the 'agayatabasa'(living in hiding)of Pandava's for one year when they came from far off Hastinapur (modern Delhi) to 'Birat Raja's state,then known as 'Matsyadesa'.Today's Mayurbhanj district & earlier Mayurbhanj Gadjat state'is known to be "Matsyadesa'of Mahabharata, as the remains of fort of Birat Raja and Kichak temple and the place in which the five Pandava's have hid their weapons, bears testimony to this place. This region left many monuments, sites to those rulers of Mahabharat era and thereafter Mughal, Maratha, British & Bhanja Kings who have mightily contributed to this region in the form of many buildings, structures, monuments, heritage sites etc.which are presently on ths ruins, due to apathetism & lack of important data, documentation on each of these sites, whose proper documentation can pave the way for its conservation & protection for humanity. The area has remained under the rule of popular Bhanja Kings for a considerable period of time who hails from Rajputana i.e. Jaipur in modern Rajasthan in 598 A.D and the first King was Maharaja Jai Singh and since than the 'Bhanja dynasty' has ruled this region with 56 successive rulers till its merger in 1949 with Indian Union and became a part of Odisha, adjacent to Bihar, Bengal & Jharkhand. The benevolent Bhanja rulers ushered the golden age during their period which was manifested in different art & architecture,monuments & buildings,temples & palaces ;a number of which have already been ruined, extincted and many such heritage sites & buildings are on the verge of fast extinction, due to the onslaught of modern construction process and growing human habitation.

Since this study also equally laid stress on the

documentation of actual sites it covers a whole gamut of areas, regions personally covered by the fellow in an intensive field study vigorously to capture those remains of Mahabharatian era. These photographic details provide more flesh to the bone- of -belief that it was the Matsyadesa and once upon a time Pandava's presence in this soil had blistered it with magnanimous power.

Due efforts have been taken to incorporate all such actual sites but inadvertent omissions if any be rectified by the Fellow-author in upcoming versions.All such sites,places,structures,monuments have been covered under 'Bhanja Vignette'.

Senior Fellow

SECTION : A

Raibania Fort

The Journey for Mahabharat era sites: An exploration which establishes a point that - Raja Biraat fort -where weapons like Arjuna's Gandiva and kichaka fort or The Pandava's undertook journey from far -off Hastinapur (present Delhi) to Matsyadesa during their sojourn of one year agayatabasa, like wise this journey of Mahabharatian site has been started from Raibania, the legendary site & remains of Raja Biraat of Mahabharat fame situated at about 36 km from Balasore, 66 km from Mayurbhanj. The area passes through famous & the only air strip of eastern India.The road from Denganalia village to the Biraat Raja's fort site of about 16 km are muddy, inaccessible & presently the Pradhanmantri gramsadak yojana is being carried out for which it is almost impossible to pass on the under-constructed road. However with much difficulty after reaching the spot,popularly known as Raibania fort here whose distance of 3 km from main road to the fort was under construction with Rs 16 lakh assistance from local MP Kharavela Swain who took the initiative during last two years to construct a pucca road known here as Gadachandi road to the fort site of this Mahabharat era.The area is surrounded by many smaller & big ponds, tanks which according to the villagers have been named such as – Kaushalya, Jaljantra, Kundigadia, Bhuynapokhari, Nandiaka, Digi.The fort bears the testimony of Biraat Raja of Mahabharat fame where the Paanch-Paandavas came to complete their 'agayatabasa'.His brother in law Raja Kichaka of Mahabharat fame had his own fort around 250 km from this place which defines this region as 'Matsyadesa'during Mahabharat era.There is a popular saying in odiya here 'kichaka bahubale Birat raja' means Biraat is king under the powerful arm, strength of his brother-in-law Kichaka.The fort is completely ruined except around 10/15 feets of boundary walls and a gate.The inside of the fort has become heaps of stones & debris depicting the unique style of those era.A spot where local people called it to be the bathing place of Maharani's have underground stairs which if undertaken can open many new insights. It is known from local gentry sources that the excavation by some officials some years back were too short & stopped due to want of funds & since than it is remaining in this stage, as several photographs depicts this. The fort is surrounded with a Devi Kichaki, the popular deity who guards the fort & anyone trying to photograph HER simply yields black on print. With local community involvement a Shiva temple is under completion.The deity has a unique major festival during Panasankranti of april 14 every year.The fort was last stated to be in possession of Rai Bahadur Singh, a zamindar of the area and thereafter it become a govt.property,but no steps were taken to declare it as a major historic heritage site, property or never undertaken by ASI or any other conservation departments for which it is further on the ruins.The local people now guards this Mahabharat era fort zone zealously and narrates many anecdotes of those days which has been enliven on hearsay like how the Pandavas took shelter at Biraat Raja, Draupadi was hiding with his queen & how Kichaka saw her feet etc to the days relates to Mahabharat era and thereafter by Maharatta's attack on this area, fort ;Kalapahad's attack on this fort & laments the vivid historicity of those days today known as Khiching on which the exploration progresses. However after the embarking of several visits by this author to the Raibania area it is found that, a group of local youths have formed a Raibania Suraksha Samity to safeguard the deteriorating fort with kolkatta's ASI being step into takeup protection,excavation work soon.

Prehistoric-Mahabharatian era site

The prehistoric Mahabharatian era site is situated in the foothills of famous Similipal sanctuary in Kaptipada subdivision-block of Podadiha Panchayat and the area is known as- Itagarh & Sanjunpal.Way back to 1995 the Archaeological Survey of India(ASI) team had undertook an excavation and curved out a number of things like iron ammunitions, iron quiver, soil-stone-iron-pots, utensils, burnt bricks etc. It was known from the locality that two former ASI officials Debendra Barik, Prasanta Ray in coordination with a retired teacher & a social orgn.- Sankarsan Pradhan & Jatiya Seba Pratisthana respectively had initiated its preliminary survey, findings. And it was during those years the author being a part of the social orgn.then had an opportunity to study it which resulted into very unique findings. It was also a popular belief among the locals here that the entire Similipal area needs to be exclusively reserve as a protected site so as to preserve many relics, things, materials of Mahabharatian era as Raja Biraat & his brother in law Kichaka's domain was found in this region and part of this area comes under it – stated many historians, researchers while depicting the Mahabharat fame 'Matsyadesa', popularly known today as Mayurbhanj. A number of representative findings, claims published documented earlier in the local language by this author have given momentum to this further exploration & study.

Prehistoric Mahabharatian era site:Sathilo

Another prehistoric Mahabharatian site Sathilo is a grampanchayat under Betnoti block in Mayurbhanj.The village is found with very ancient sites of ruin of a fort.These ruinous fort has been covered with two ponds from each of its sides.It was stated by village elders that there was a fort along with a temple worshipped by some rulers belongs to Bhanja kings although many contest this view. However few years ago the local population on their own initiatives have digged the area and found some stone slabs having artistic figures, curvings, images of deities like Durga, Nursingha, SriKrishna and kept those in a local temple.Today the ruinous of the said area has completely razed to the ground and the entire heritage area has been densely populated with number of houses.The particular site of the ruinous fort has been now under the occupation of one Nilakantha Mohapatra who said he has purchased this piece of land from one Bengali, Mani Babu long ago on inquiry by the author.However here is no remnants of fort except some land level bricks and the entire heritage zone was never excavated by Archaeological Survey of India (ASI) and thus a gorgeous heritage site on the route to Kolkata-Chennai highway has gone into memory of public minds in this locality.

Probable Pre-historic Mahabharatian sites

Mayurbhanj state otherwise famous as Matsyadesa of Mahabharat period houses many historic,heritage sites and after much research a view on this subject ,numbers of such sites were enlisted.Many such historic-heritage sites dating back to stone age,prehistoric age,monolithic period donot have any remains although some have few important relics & remains to boost such claims viz; Khiching, Pratappur, Muruda, Kaptipada, Baidipur, Bahlda, Kuchei, Mahulia, Deosole, Bisoi, Dahikothi sasan, Ambdali sasan, Mananda, Amsikd, Jadipal to name a few.Such places have been glorify by their ancientness & possession of many heritageness like unique culture,art,crafts,designwares etc.The study has charted out all such heritage sites after taking primay observation from different quarters .

Itagarh, Dubigarh-Mahabharatian era sites

The famous Mahabharatian era sites where remains,cultural folklore especially of the agayatabasa(hideout)of Paandavas is famous in this region.Interestingly the author since long have come across through many such materials from the few short stories & folklores from the elders.But during the course of this study it has been crystal clear that Paandava's during their agayatabasa of one year came from

Hastinapur,Kurukshetra(modern Delhi region) to hide themselves in such a way that for one full year,the Kaurava's could not recognize them and incase they have been recognized or identified by them during this period,they would again have to go to vanavasa for another twelve years. Such crucial condition in their victory might have forced the Pandava's to far off places like Matsyadesa or popularly known today as Mayurbhanj.Accordingly Paandvas redesignted themselves as follows to reach this place which was ruled by then valiant ruler Kichaka and his brother in law Raja Biraat.Yudhistira named himself as Kanka-a Brahmin;Bhima known as Ballabha,the cook;Arjuna as Bruhannalla-the music teacher;Nakula the Ashwapalak as horse care taker,Sahadev as Gopala,the caretaker of cows in the palace of king Biraat and Draupadi as Sudeshna/Sairindhri,the courtesan to Maharani of Biraat Raja.It is a rare opportunity to visit this palace site of Biraat Raja which is popularly known here as Dubigarh(immersed fort) & Itagarh(fort of bricks). This place is just exists in the foothills of famous Similipal sanctuary & biosphere reserve. Dubigarh is inside the curvical mountaneous range of Similipal. The locals stated that there is a walkable route to Dubigarh but it is very tedious, dangerous as it is in the hilltop. They further said that Dubigarh was once the palace of Raja Biraat who gave shelter to the Paandavs during their agayatabasa of a year. There was a huge place which lateron with the passage of time have been covered under stone heaps, thick bushes & jungles of different kinds.In the opposite sides of Biraat's palace two ponds popularly known as Raja & Rani pokhari is found even today which were perhaps used by kings &

queens respectively.Despite the best of efforts it could not possible to reach the exact location of Dubigarh inview of big stone slabs & attempting to reach the exact spot to capture the Biraat-gada (fort). However a number of photographs of this place from a distance were captured which gives a shape to the existing footway to the palace area. Just below it, on the ground level is situated Itagarh where a small village & an ashram school exists. Just adjacent to the ashram school there are cultivable lands and the village elders took the fellow-author amidst their land to the exact point where 15 years ago the ASI undertook an excavation but since then left this work midway which has gradually covered up with muds,bushes,grass fields. In this excavation of ASI there was some remains found dating back to Mahabharatian era according to many historian.The area is famous as Itagarh where bricks of unusual size was used as in Haripur fort.The elders said that, the entire area if excavated would give new meanings to Mahabharatian era proofs which was abandoned due to huge expenses.The area has been documented with several photographs.

Mahabharatian era site: Sami-brukhya

Perhaps this particular site speaks the story of Paandava's agayatabasa stay, as many remains, cultural folklores of their weapons hiding in this particular place known as Sami-brukhya exhibits. It is situated around 12 km from the fort of Biraat Raja near Dubigarh.Infact Itagarh, Dubigarh forts which are situated in the foothills of famous Similipal sanctuary is the region where Samibrukhya falls. Situated on the river bed of Kushabhadra in Radho village of Podadiha under Udala subdivision, this spot exudes a mystery of heritageness along with a sense of presence of mighty Paandava's. When one reaches the village Kulialam a narrow road greets the visitors to take into this mysterious zone upto river Kushabhadra where a matha' situated.There is no permanent bridge over this river and during Makar-sankranthi a big mela of local community is organized on the past glory of pandava's which lasts upto a fortnight.The pathways from the riverbed to Samibrukhya is tedious,rocky and muddy which is around one km.and this Mahabharatian era heritage site has filled one with a sense of awe,air of mystery & spine chilling visuals,as if the paandva's are greeting with their holy presence.

Samibrukhya,the odiya translation of a particular tree where the Paandava's reportedly hid their weapons & armoury during agayatabasa, on the core of this big tree,is no more a tree today.As elders since generations have gathered many anecdotes pass on to their future generation about the pandavas arms hiding tree which has turned today into a big rocky mountain with thousands of trees sprouted from this holy mountaneous range.Visitors,tourists have been able to ride on upto an extent of this tree-turned-mountain which is very difficult to climb.There are many folklores among the locality that,the particular spot of the tree-core where pandavas hided their arms were always guarded by poisonous big snakes of mammoth size as described in scriptures but never seen to bare eyes of human beings. During field visits to this area it has been covered with number of photo-documntation featue and found that many small caves have developed encompassing this tree-mountain range and possibly such hideous places inside in this hilly forest range be used by paandava's during Mahabharat era.

Kulialam Matha & Basudev Temple

The presence of Kulialam-math where Basudev Temple (Shri Krishna) just beneath this Samibrukhya, a range further connotes & establish the presence of Shri Krishna & Panchu-Paandava's. As usually this area has been infested with many deities, mostly Goddess, but here in this particular spot it is amazing to find a Shri Krishna-Basudev place of worship. This matha is also famous as polar worship place of pandava's. Elders,researchers and stories lend support to the view that,the paandava's came from Hastinapur on agayatabasa from one corner to another,i.e,from one polarity to another and perhaps they might have renamed this place which was ideal for their hiding,even today also and as they were great worshippers of Lord Shri Krishna,they had built this Basudev temple in this polarity, known as kulialam matha.The place is very calm,serene and one would instantly feel the presence of paandava's and their mentor Sri Krishna, as if one is getting drown into the Mahabharat-past zone.This matha is guarded by a sadhu known as Jaganath Das who worship the Basudeva everyday.The demand for better management of this Mahabharatian era matha has been vested with a trust board and the subcollector,Udala is its executive officer which looks after its management.But seeing things as they are ,one would easily find a conclusion that,the officials didn't gave the shrine the needed care nor funds for which it looks dilapidated.The matha has few acres of landed property and its harvest annually is the only continuous source of income for the nitipuja of deity.The only other occasion it receives dakshina is when Makarsankranthi sets in. A former local MP has given 2.50 lakh for construction of a storehouse which is used as police outpost during the mela and round the year it houses the paddy,rice of the matha poperty.The photographing details of this place filled one with a sense of connectedness to the pristine past,heritageous glory of this Mahabharatian era site.A report published by this author has given the locals perception that this heritage site is gradually sinking down the Kushabhadra river and the matter was takenup for road-bridge in this area and NABARD has agreed to pledge around 1.60 Crore for construction of bridge on river Kushabhadra,thus directly connecting to this Mahabharat era heritage relics.

Mahabharatian heritage: Kainsari Fort

A visit to Kainsari rea where once a fort was built of the Mahabharatian era bears a mystical testimonyeven to this day .The Bhanja rulers have constructed a number of forts in the glory of their scions and to uphold royalty and one such remnants is Kainsari Fort. The fort was dating back to Raja -Biraat of Mahabharat fame. Many elders believe and it has pass on to generation that, it was the Capital of Raja Biraat of Mahabharat fame. The areas situated in present Udala subdivisions. Many also believes that this area was once the penance-ashram of famous sage of Mahabharat, Uddalaka, from which the present day name of Udala derived. The Fellow during the interaction with local elders at Kainsari chronicled that – this was the place of famous Mahabharatian sage Uddalaka as well as the Capital of Raja Biraat. This fort was enjoyed by second line royalty of Bhanja kings having the title of 'sai' or 'das' who usually accompany the surname Biraat Raja, for instance one of the name of princely rulers was – Nanu Sai Biraat Raja, Shatrughan Das Biraat Raja. It gives one a very amazing feelings that the rulers of this fort was adding a suffix 'Biraat Raja' with their names which was nowhere found in this region or any other region of India. This signifies that they were the descendants of Raja Biraat, who were adding the suffix of Raja Viraat with their names.

The fort site was located amidst a narrow village road and at the end of village jungle one finds the remnants of a fort. The entire fort area has been covered under heaps of clay and a hilly-top look is found except the edges of old boundary wall. Here is a 'gada-chandi devi' as was worshipped in all the forts of Mahabharatian era which is also worshipped now. The entire fort area was donated some years back by the descendants of Nanusai Viraat Raja family to govt. which has constructed & running the Kainsari primary school. Instead of fighting for the fort-land, we donate it for greater public cause to that of imparting primary education to the less privileged children in this area, said Shatrughan Das Babu Viraat Raja, who prefers to drop the suffix of Viraat Raja from his name and simply like to call him in his name. This means gradually the descendants of Raja Viraat feels to drop this surname in this stiff competitive world where Values and cultures are no longer worshipped unless humanity faces major hurdles. The descendants are poor but having the dignity of their great predecessor Raja Viraat and still manages the Dalimbeswar Mahadev temple built by some of their ancestors. The photo documentation a number of historic yet ravaged area from this Kainsari fort site which reminds one the glorious past of yester years, on this Bhanja lands. The presence of Mahabharatian era culture has another substance one can find in the recently made demands of several political parties of this region. Mayurbhanj-the state was merged in 1949 with Indian Union and after 60 years of its annexation, it is deprived and undeveloped in every sector; blame it to its poor leadership or stepmotherly treatment that demands for its further division in separate districts and later on for curvingout the Viraat-state was a interesting phenomena. Because such political demands have different undertones but in this region, there is a demand for Viraat-state, which indicates that there is presence of Mahabharatian era heritages, cultures, and Viraat Raja, a tangible testimony to the subtle evidences.

Mahabhartian era site: Dhudeswarpitha-Baruni- Khunta

Another important Mahabharatian era relics is the place popularly known as Dhudeswar-pitha or Dhudeswar baruni.It is nearby to Khunta block bazaar in Mayurbhanj district or the pristine Matsyadesa of Mahabharat fame.The area comprises of Ghantasila mountain range wherein legends & relics shows that several mountaineous rocks having imprints of the knee mark of mighty Bhima. This mountain also have a number of relics of Arjuna's footprints searching for arrows according to many elders. The area is said to be habitated by mighty Paandava's during their one year agayatabasa in this Matsyadesa. Dhudeswar is the name of Lord Shiva here which houses this Mahabharatian era relics in its stones, jungles & rocky mountains and stories of culturally inherited generationswise about many myths of Paandava's sojourn in this Matsyadesa region. Situated in the bordering villages of Sankhunta, Titia, Bhandgaon comprises this famous Pannadava's legendary place nearby which river Gangahaar is flowing.The Shiva, believed to be appeared on this rocky river bed of Gangahaar which hides it round the year inside the rocks except during Baruni-snan',makar sankranti and to have a darshan'on this auspicious day believing they would attain moksha' on this day. Apart from Dhudeswar barunipitha this Mahabharatian era relics also houses some other important tourists places such as Delingi -bandha, Mahimadharma Sunya mandir on Tangrahudi(name of a mountain),centennial Nrusingha Baba Mahima ashram near Naluha river on this scenic spot which immediately transport a visitor to the era of Mahabharat with the several myths of mighty Paandava's.This site has remained under complete oblivion from visitors eye so far as illegal mining activities have already damaged major portion of this historic mountaneous range believed to be blessed with the marks of mighty Paandava's -Bhima & Arjuna's physical strength as well as serenity.

Mahabharatian interaction

The attempt to bring back the ancient memory of this Matsyadesa of Mahabharat fame, presently named as Mayurbhanj, the Fellow had interacted with two scholars in this regard and brought the ambience of Mahabharat fame matsyadesa which is symmetrically manifesting on observance of folklore, physical structures along with repleting memory of localities. The biggest discovery is: there is an area known as Paanch-pidh which is locally known as 'village for five' which have villages/areas in the names of Paanch-pandavas of Mahabharat fame. These are Arjuna-pidh or village-Arjuna Judhistir-pidh, Bhim-pidh etc which many believes that, perhaps habitated by the Paandavs during their agyaat -basa to this region, far away from Hastinapur. However no scholars or researchers of repute have worked upon this idea so far which is gaining strengthen with evidences of Paandavas- agyaatbasa period in this matsyadesa - Mayurbhanj.

Paanchpidh – Abode of Paandavas

The several field visits undertook for research-visits to a number of places, replete with Mahabharatian era glories & having tangible existence of evidences largely associated with Paandavas. In this Matsyadesa of Mahabharat era fame today known as Mayurbhanj, Here is a region popularly known as Paanch-pidh i.e, places of five which gives historical justification as well as evidences of Mahabharatian era, more specifically the period of agyaatbasa of panchu-paandavas. As stated earlier the Paandavas along with Draupadi came to this region, then the Raja Biraat's kingdom & Kichaka's palaces and hid their weapons in a mountain named Samibrukhya. The region where Paandavas were staying, came to be famous & known as paanch-pidh,the place of five which today also bears this name and panchpidh is a subdivision under this present Mayurbhanj district .The most famous heritage site in this region is Kichaka's fort,the deity called Kichakeswari .This area is popularly known as Khiching today which earlier knew as Khijingkota .The Bhanja rulers have had their kingdom in this place earlier, which was later on shifted to Haripur and thereafter to Baripada's Belgadia palace which today stands as a testimony to this historic-heritage sites. Panchpidh today comprises of a total five blocks viz; Karanjia, Jashipur, Thakurmunda, Raruan & Sukruli .It has a total of sixty gram panchayats & one NAC in Karanjia, the sub-divisional headquarter. The area is thickly populated by tribes like, santhal, bathudi, bhumija, kohl, gond and their major vocation is agriculture, cattle rearing & collection of minor forest products, as this region is a thickly forest land. This region is the last connecting point of Paandavas journey as they started from Raja Biraat's fort from Raibania to Shamibrukhya in Podadiha-Udala-than to Dubigarh-Itagarh in the similipal region then passed enroute in Sarat-Thakurmunda to Karanjia-Khiching otherwise famous as panchpidh region.

Many historians, researchers also earlier indicated about this, but the field study of this Fellow amply proves this point that from Raibania's Raja Biraat fort to Kichak's fort at panchpidh is a contigous route used by the pandaavas during their agayaatbasa after their defeat in the game of dice. The relics, antics, places of interests has amply proved this which during the field study found that – the Bhanja rulers like Kota Bhanj, Diga Bhanj, Rana Bhanj were fond of subtle art works which was promoted by them during their ruling years. In these period of 10/11 century the famous temple of Khiching was built up by the Bhanjas .At that time they were worshipping Buddha & Buddhist idol Abolkiteswara is found here in the temple. The remains of Biraat & Kichaka's fort was found in on the verge of complete extinction. The copper coins, plates and materials derived from the archaeological renovation few years back proves the point that – during Mahabharatian era the fort of Raja Biraat was found in the bank of river Bhandan and that of Kichaka's in the bank of river Khairi. Thus the two famous river 'khairi-bhandan' emerges from this region. Here also once the famous pet tigress khairi was found .The area was having the remains of some symbols, remnants of fort-walls, gadakhai (a watery circle built up by kings then from immediate enemy attack) and the Rajguru, Rani-gadhua pond also today stands to remind one the glory & grandeur of Mahabharatian era. This region was first excavated by Ley

Tikkel during 1840 and thereafter the famous archaeologist Mr Begler visited it during 1874-76 when he found the famous temple and several stone curved idols were scattered everywhere and the initial attempt to collect these were takenup. Again in 1907-08 the Great Maharaja Shri Ramchandra BhanjDeo invited the archaeologist Nagendranath Basu who made some effort to realign the dilapidated region. Again in 1922-23 Maharaja Purnachandra BhanjDeo has assigned the revival work to Rai Bahadur Ramprasad Chandra, than the superintendent of Calcutta Museum who was instrumental in renovating, discovering, replacing and realigning many rare idols of ancient era curved with such architectural marvel which is difficult to get even today. This proves the love of maharaja's for fine arts- crafts and idol worshipping. During the period of Maharaja Pratap Chandra BhanjDeo the 75 feet height temple of Khiching was realigned with ancient engravings by noted archaeologist Birbal Bose & Parmananda Acharya which took this new shape by 1940. This heritage piece have identical curvature with the famous Brahmeswara temple of Brahmeswarapatna in todays Bhubaneswar. These heritage sites gives evidences to several aspects then found by the patron –kings like Buddhism, Jainism and some rare forms of deities like, upward lingeswara, astabhuja Durga, ardha-narishwar, dancing Ganesha, apsaras, kartikeswara on mayura etc. The art-crafts of this famous Khiching temple is unique in the entire eastern India. Its presiding deity Khijingeswar is stated to be sitting naked on a corpse which except the pujak no one has seen nor permitted to witness since the days of Bhanjas.

The scholar-Fellow covered this famous heritage site along with few Engravings of statues, idols recovered from the debris of forts earlier on several occasions.

Benu Madhab Math : Paandava's place of worship

The exploration proceeded with the study of Mahabharatian era Matsyadesa with greater depths had connected the rich, resplendent region of nature from many historians, researchers of past who has some or other way worked in this region, on subjects other than this. The famous such persons were Nilamani Senapati, S.N. Sarkar, J.K. Sahu, Dr K.C. Panigrahi, Dr H.K. Mahatab, Janmejay Sahu, P.K. Dash to name a few who have depicted the place & region in their writings as a natures gift to world, but many have unable to draw such similarities of Mahabharatian era relics, except in an sporadic manner. As stated earlier the area in Raruan where Sahadeva & Nakula were looking after the cow-cattles of Raja Biraaat is a fertile land where crops grow immensely and the people were fond of eking out their living out of cattle rearing & grazing. Apart from a little distance of Biraat fort in Khiching comes the natures paradise, Similipal sanctuary. The Panch Paandavas were stated to be accompanying Raja Biraat during his 'mrigayaa' or hunting spree to this region. The Pandava's along with Sairindri or Draupadi were also accompanying Raja Biraat & his queen Sudeshna during their hunting and legend established that there is a BeniMadhb math-temple in this deep, dense forest zone and which probably they were worshipping. Because under what circumstances a Krishna or BeniMadhab temple was constructed by whom, & when is still an enigma. As the Paandavas were the sakha's and the worshipper of Lord Krishna, they have devoted their stay in worshipping HIM in this thick forest secretly. The area now is under reserve forest division of Similipal Authority. The Fellow also consulted with some elders about this and they had also substantiated this view that, when there is no population movement nor it falls on the usual human habitat route this might have built by the Paandavas.

Mahabharatian Heritage : Kichakeswari Temple

A number of cultural heritage sites dating back to Mahabharatian era as the local myths & tales depict the site and events. Raja Kichaka, the brother–in-law of famous Viraat-Raja of Mahabharata fame had his capital at Khijingkota, as known to historians and today it is famous as Khiching and its presiding deity called Kichakeswari. It was believed that Kichakeswari was the presiding deity of Bhanja kings and in a number of places the idols of Maa Kichakeswari was found. In the Mayurbhanj palace itself, the western gate of the palace was the entry point of Maa Kichakeswari and it was closely worshipped by Bhanja kings exclusively by them only and outsiders were not allowed inside the temple. It is said that the temple Goddess was very effective (pratakhya)to the prayers of kings who inturn worship Her everyday and on some special occasions like, leading the armed forces on victory mission. The temple during the occasion of dussehra had witnessed large number of animal sacrifice including buffalo in its precincts which the royalty was fond of, to appease the deity. This palace temple was first opened to general public by Maharaja Pratap Chandra BhanjDeo during late 60's.Thereafter it was opened for all the time. The morning & evening worship bell of the temple reverberetes the whole palace precincts which several students used to witnessed as the palace was turned into a college by the Maharaja Purnachandra BhanjDeo. The temple has entry door like the Mughal era sculpture and its nata-mandap is like Hindu temple. The place where animals were sacrificed on tying on their heads has still withstood the time, engraving the blood of animal sacrifice, a saga of royalty.

The Kichakeswari Devi is the presiding deity of Bhanja kings till date and after the merger of Mayurbhanj state in 1949,its precincts was gradually diminished of celebrations like nitipuja, animal sacrifice etc for a longtime for dire want of funds and absence of royal patronage. But the present Maharaja Praveen Chandra BhanjDeo took a special interest in bringing back its past glory and accordingly reconstruction work begun and it has restored to its former glory. Now it performs its nitipuja and is open for public all the time. It has been covered with a number of photographs of this unique Mahabharatian era temple.

Region of Five : Paanchpidh

The Fellow continues with his study on the rare aspects of management of heritage sites dating back to Mahabharatian era in this matsya-desa region & more particularly in the Paanchpidh.-the Land of Five, in other words of Panchu-Paandavas. The mighty Paandavas spent their agyaatbasa in this Biraat & Kichaka Rajas region which is still an area of dense forest with mny mysterious places, signs, symbols, anecdotes dating back to Mahabharatian era. A major aspect of it is the area/region has always claim to be an important places since Mahabharatian era and is the legendary Matsyadesa,where shelters in disguise was extended to Paandavas by Biraat

Raja of Mahabharat fame. The Paandavas lived on disguise in the form of cook, cowherd, musice teacher etc and served in the aja Biraat's kingdom. Todays Raruan & Jashipur blocks area captured,registers a number of anecdotes since Mahabharatian era. The Paandavas were very active & dynamic and scholars maintains that the area of Raruan & its people are very dynamic & active and their only means of livelihood is : agriculture & cattle rearing. Nakula, one of the paandavas had reportedly spent his major times tilling the land and grazing the cow,cattles in this particular area. this is believed by many elders and it was Nakula's ideals of promotion of agricultue & cattlegrazing, rearing that majority still works on his founded ideology in this area .The Mahabharitian scriptures also maintains that Raja Biraat had entrusted these duties to Nakula. The area & many of its region which we today called Raruan block has been partly ceded to Bihar & Jharkhand state. In 1949 when Sareikela & Kharswan region was given from ex-Mayurbhanj state, its major area or popularly those known as Mahabharatian heritage sites has been adjoined to neighbouring Jharkhand area.. There was a village named Benisagar which was earlier in Matsyadesa or Mayurbhanj but this heritage place Benisagar janpad (village) is now in Jharkhand state. The Mahabharat scriptures indicates that in a big pond in this village while Draupadi was taking bath her long jumbled hair in local language- beni was sink in this pond which was lateron given to the name of this village surrounded this area; hence the area is famous as Benisagar. This area further have another pond famous as ' Keshari Kund'. Nakula, Sahadeva, and others were usually taking bath in this pond. The citizens & society in this matsyadesa region had high regard & reverence and more particularly to Paandavas, because the localities here though didn't knew that these were Paandavas but they believed them to be something of special status and left this pond for their exclusive use; hence this pond was named as Keshari kund or Royal-pond. The locals still today elieves that deities use this pond hence they desist it from using it commoly. This pond & its adjacent area witnessed a Biraat -Mela or gala festival a the time of Makar sankranthi every ear, when thousands thronged to visit, worship the place by immersing in the pond. Those immersed on this pond in this particular day are stated to be reach the glory of their life & career. In other words those taking a dip on it would become the possessor of many unique quality & power. People here worship Maa Bhairavi- the deity and here sacrificial of animal is a taboo. He Raruan block is also otherwise popularly known as Nakulapidha-the region of Nakula. Many scholars claims that its ancient name on the versatile paandavas Nakula is largely a derivative of this region – Nakulapidha which also proves that unless Nakula was habitated it once, how this area cameup with this name in this thick tribal region.

Khiching : Cultural-Geograhic boundaries

This Paandavas infested region of Raruan in Panchpidh subdivision where the famous khiching temple stood. This heritage ancient temple's construction style is similar to Brahmeswara & Lingaraj temples of Bhubaneswar as its symmetry, aestheticness, beauty, curvatures reminds one the application of similar crafts in both these temples. Khiching- the region of Biraat & Kichaka where Paandavas used to hide themselves for a year was rippled with many tales,sites of Mahabharatian days,is a region to be preserved its heritage beauty but the management of cultural geographical boundaries has put this heritage cultural institution again into a fresh controversy. The issue starts when some locals found that the management responsibility of Khiching & its temples,museum is handed over to nearby Keonjhar district culture official department instead of Mayurbhanj, to which it belongs. The area is in the Mayurbhanj district and situated in Panchpidh which is nearer to Jharkhand on one side & Keonjhar on another side. Since generations the area, geography & heritage sites were under the direct control of Bhanja rulers which after the merger of Mayurbhanj state with Odisha found to be a district and this heritage site was managed under its culture officer. But how, why & when its management responsibility has been shifted to nearby district and under what context is beyond the understanding of all. Hence local population here agitated with such geographical transference of the govt. and even submitted memorandum to hon'ble Governor of Odisha. The Fellow also published the locals sentiments and urged the govt. to restore its status as before. Cultural & Heritage Institutions transgresses all geographical boundaries and belongs to all humanity and restricting it for a certain area, region or under certain control bound to generate heated sentiments.

Khiching was the ancient capital of Bhanja rulers where Mahabharat fame Biraat -gada(fort) was found to be stood once in the periphery of Bhandan river.The copper plate inscription, archaeological excavations and the artifacts found from this region proves this. Amidst thick jungles two rivers – khairi & Bhandan, the forts of Biraat & Kichaka was stood once as its remains were found for years after the merger of Mayurbhanj-matsyadesa. In the year 1907-08 Maharaja Sri Ramchandra Bhanjdeo invited the noted archaeologist Nagendranath Basu from Kolkata to excavate the ancient sites which found several such heritage monuments then. Again in 1922-23 during the reign of Maharaja Sri Purnachandra BhanjDeo this site was again explored by Rai Bahadur Ramprasad Chandra, then superintendent of Indian Museum at Kolkata. Hundreds of ancient monuments, idols, artifacts were recovered from the damaged fort sites at Khiching and stored in the local museum here. Lateron Maharaja Pratapchandra BhanjDeo had entrusted the replication & renovation of famous Kichakeswari temple of Khiching by entrusting the work to archaeologist Paramananda Acharya which was completed by 1940. The 75 feet tall Khiching temple combines the ancient Mahabharatian art in numbers of its found idols such as : shiva, dancing Ganesha, Ardhanarishwara ,Asthabhuja Durga, Urdha-lingeswara etc. Khiching is one of the major shakti pitha' and people of all the religions, castes ranging from Brahmin, harijan, adivasi used to directly worship the deity. The community of stonework artisans is a rare community here on whose development the Scholar-Fellow has submitted a proposal to revive, popularize their unique art traditions to the newly formed State Institute for Arts & Crafts Development during this study. A writeup on the khiching of the scholar is also published highlighting several unique aspects of this Mahabharatian era heritage sites is given for better understanding.

Khijjinga Kotta Mandal & Modern Khiching:

The Importance of this heritage place could well be imagined when the Central govt. has included this place under its Rural Tourism Development Programme in Odisha alongwith seven other such heritage sites. The scholar-fellow launch a study on the trends and it is found that eight heritage-tourists spots like Konarka, Raghurajpur alongwith Khiching was extended with 4 Crore grant each of which would earmarked with 50 Lakhs of allocation to be spent for development of these heritage villages under Rural Tourists development Fund. But strangely except two projects – Konarka, Raghurajpur the rest village tourists programme was not even taken up even after four years of its sanction & there is chances that, the allotted amount may taken back by the Centre. When asked about non-expenses of the central govt. grant, the tourism department.has several reasons to offered like: the task was entrusted to INTACH and after two years they now back from this programme. Similarly the SIDAC-State Institute for Development of Arts & Crafts was entrusted a part of this work but except issuing an advertisement for documenting stone arts curvings, it has so far not done anything concrete. These reasons have so far proved the inability in spending the huge grant allotted by Centre even after a lapse of four years, although stoneware artisans are facing fund crunch to improve their crafts & livelihood. As stated earlier, the adjacent village – Keshna nearest to Khiching is a village of heritage & crafts and requires fund support for its overall development but no such govt. programme has been launched although many craftsman's are leaving these traditional Art & crafts thus depriving the posterity about the rich heritageness of a place !

Many historians,researchers however subscribe to the view that,Kotta Bhanja is the founder of KhijjingKotta –one of the earliest known historical rulers of Bhanja dynasty of Khijjing. The copper-plate grants of Rama Bhanja mentions the year of 188 & 193 as an unspecified era,which probably was the 'Bhauma era'started in 736 & 929 AD. Thus it may be reasonably concluded that Kotta Bhanja-the grand father of Rama Bhanja flourished in the 9th century AD. Even he was restyled his name as 'Rajadhiraj' in the copper-plate grants. This Khijjing-mandala or modern Khiching is a region enriched in art, culture, aesthetics and exudes a rare charm of heritageness as one observes the archaeological remains, sites in this Mahabharatian era -Matsyadesa. British historians Lt.Tikkel & Beglar visited this region in 1240 & 1674 AD respectively. Khiching had originally a group of temples of which the main temple was that of Shiva - as the Bhanja Kings were Saivites and the Bhanja copper plate grants open with an invocation to Lord Shiva. Khiching was a 'Astayana Shaiva Kshetra' meaning Eight Linga's Place, were enshrined in eight temples. Today also one can see seven lingas at this place and the eighth one has been removed to Kesharibeda, the neighbourhood of Khiching. Three temples are still in sight at Khiching —Kutai Tundi is the oldest as its date of construction is assessed as 9th century AD. It was restored and reconstructed by Durbar Administration. The main temple, the presiding deity-Khijjingeswari has striking similarities with the temple of Brahmeswara of Bhubaneswar. This templ was buried under a mound on which stood a small brick temple of Khijjingeswari and an unfinished temple called Khandia-deula'. Maharaja Pratap Chandra & Purna Chandra Bhanj Deo took active steps to restore & renovate these oldest temples of Khiching under the supervision of Ram Prasad

Chand alongwith Parmananda Acharya, Sailendranath Basu all archaeologists of repute.

The site museum at Khiching houses a large numbers of idols as per Hindu tradition found during excavation at different sites. The museum was organized in 1922 by R P Chand and is the largest Museum in Orissa with a collection of antiquities like – Stone sculptures, Lithic Implements, Beads, Pottery, Copper Plates & Sanads. After merger of Mayurbhanj state, a number of important artifacts from this museum was taken by Govt. of Odisha to state museum at Bhubaneswar, where it is now found and this museum left with few materials. Its management handed over to nearest Keonjhar district authorities has again earned the wreaths of locals and it is closed since last one & half years.

Though basically a Shaivaite establishments, the excavations during periods found large numbers of Sakta, Saura, Vaishnaba, Ganpatya tradition aplenty. It was observed that, there was fine blending of different religious cultures at Khiching under the royal patronage of Bhanja's. A major departure in Khiching's temples have – here no Mukhasala (frontage) or Natmandir is found. This same style was found in Brahmeswara at Bhubaneswar, Benisagar, Khekpatra, Anjan at Jharkhand, Bankura in Midnapore of West Bengal, Simdega in Bihar.

The Mahabharatian remains of two ancient forts – Biraatgarh & Kichakgarh (fort) were also found at Khiching few years back is now only houses the main temple. A Buddhist stupa with a casket and ashes was also discovered at Khiching ,as reported in the ASI Annual Reports in the year 1922 to 1925. Another very important aspect of Khiching was – it synthesise the Hindu &

Adivasi culture,as here both the culture have merged. The temple is worshipped both by Hindu Brahmins & Adivasi-Bhuyan and it is always open for Hindus,Dalits,adivasis & every caste of people. Every year a big mela is held here during the Sivaratri festival when large numbers of pilgrims gather here to worship Kichakeswari and Nilakantheswara-Shiva close to the temple compound.

Keshna – derivative of Krishna'

A derivative from Krishna-Draupadi is the name of this village in this Paanchpidh region. The area is habitated mostly by stone curving artisans and its stone works are famous allover. The artistry on stone & its heritageness bears the testimony of a community which was famous for their artistry on stone. Draupadi was fell in love with these crafts, legends maintains. In ancient period the name of this area was Krishna-another name of Draupadi. Many villagers here feels that the present name of Keshna was largely derives from Krishna, otherwise why in a tribal region a village in the name of Draupadi caught the attention of villagers ,is stated to be due to Paandavas habitation once.

Similarly a little distance from Raja Biraat 's gada-fort there is also a village Pandurasila. In this area comparatively richer castes of kuber & gauda, a cattle rearing community one can found. The name of this village as Paandavsila was perhaps its earlier name which was lateron derivated as pandurasila. This Pandurasila or Pandavsila area is also popularly famous as Judhistirapidh, the eldest of Paandav as his superiority runs supreme in this region once, during their stay it is believed by local villagers, elders, researchers, historians. Interestingly numerous heritage sites, areas, villages, places clearly depict this region as Paandavas visited place once and it corroborates all the symptoms of Matsyadesa as described in Mahabharat.

The queen along with her group of beauty maidens & Paanchali used to took bath in this water reservoir, away from commonmen's sight.It was once during her bath that Draupadi lost her 'beni''(hair) in this lake hence this name-Benisagar. The lake situated in a sylvan surroundings even today, quite away from public gaze. The entire area is covered with tall Sal trees, the hallmark of Mayurbhanj forests, where one could find a big dam like facilities have been erected. Just infront of this water pond one found the excavations of a big fort is in the process since last three years.The excavated materials include stonewares, idols builtup of black-mugni stones akin to the stone crafts of khiching. A number of Shivalingas are also found in this excavations for which it led to believe that, perhaps after secretely taking bath, the queensfolk used to worship Shiva in this temple. The excavation is in progress presently by ASI, Ranchi circle and a number of idols have been recovered in this region. But sadly the area once habitated in Mayurbhanj is now in Jharkhand. The Fellow – asked about it and got the reply that,it was very much a part of Jharkhand.Hence the forthcoming generations might never believe that it was once a part of matsyadesa –due to this political & administrative divisions, leading towards cultural bifurcation.A big museum of ASI is also under construction process and house all those excavated rare ancient materials, recovered during these digging.The quality of bricks used in these excavated fort-temple is similar to that of Haripur & Khiching –rectangular in shape but thickness is less than todays bricks.The scholar-fellow took few snaps of this place ideal for meditation as tranquility rules here but was prevented by the ASI staffs, not to photographed as it is in progress. However three photographs was already taken which are given herewith.

Keshna – Abode of Krishna'

Draupadi whose other name is Krishna was assigned this village situated just four km.from famous khiching temple after one crosses Ghikhali village on the roadside.Both the side of road one could witness a number of stoneware artisans are busy in ripping the black mugni stones and out of it, they used to design various eyecatching stonecrafts-idols of different kinds,animals other household useable items are being forked out from these stones.Around 200 craftsman lives in this area alone of which 300 are households.Almost all the major adults are being trained to become a craftsman of stone artistry,but with days passed however their number started receding as new generes are opting jobs outside this traditional mode of earning. The villagers believed that their village keshna have a never ending supply of black-mugni stone out of which they used to earn their livelihood since generations. This black mugni stone is widely used in construction of famous khiching temple once.The villagers are proud of their crafts and is lamenting on the resource crunch in this stone arts & crafts.Few years ago a bank and a non-govt.orgn.has organized a workshop to build the capacities of stone crafts but greater efforts with funds to improve their skill, living is needed in this Mahabharatian site.Few photographs taken by the scholar of this area are given.

Biraat Sena- Mahabharatian relics

The existence of Biraat sena in this Mahabharatian famous matsydesa signifies that,Raja Biraat belongs to this region and interestingly a troupe called "Biraat sena" is in existence since long.They might have ascendants to the members of Biraat-sena(military) community.This sena very oftenraised the demand for a Biraat state for the community of Mahanta's who are neither tribals nor general- their physical features are sharp, tallsome of their habits are similar to local tribes & some are like general higher castes.They might have descendants of Biraat Raja's army,believes many,as a number of material evidence signifies that like their lifestyles, their taste for superior quality,their demand from exclusion from ST list before independence & now for reinclusion in this same list, their livelihood pattern mostly by cultivation, cow, cattle rearing & dependence on agriculture etc.

Bhima's Relics in Matsyadesa :

The Scholar-Fellow came across through few relics of Bhima - the Great Paandavas during their sojourn here in this Biraatdesa or Mahabharata fame Matsyadesa. Two relics are of much importance- Dhudhua in Kaptipada subdivision & Bhimkund near Thakurmunda under Karanjia or Panchpir (five-owners place) believed to be designated on the great Paandavas.

Dhudhua or Durudha is a hillock in Badkhunta in Kaptipada subdivision .Here is a waterfall whose sound goes to distant places. & Its name is derived from this sound – dhu, dhu. This hillock area is about five acres & in its south lies a pool of water which connects to the river – Gangahara. The pool from which this waterfall is known as 'Gauri-patta' containing a Swambhu-linga (nature made Shivalinga) wherein a big pool called 'Rohini-Kunda which witness a big mela every Baruni-day – during Shivaratri. In its east lies a hillock famous as 'Ghatsila. Here in a cave, the image of four armed goddess called Lakhai-handi is represented with a goat & a lion under her left and right feet .Few yards from this cave lies an oval stone which local here called 'Khuda-putuli' as it is popularly believed that the Great Bhima pressed his knees on this stone as the impressions are still visible on it. Ruins of three brick built temples was found earlier in three different places of Ghatsila earlier; which now is completely damaged. This ancient heritage site has been in a ruinous condition due to years of neglect by the local authorities opined a number of elders in this village.

Bhimkund

Another relics attributed to mighty Bhima is a large and deep pool of the Baitarani river in Thakurmunda region in Panchpir subdivision. The legend established that Bhima – the second of Paandavas used to take his baths here in this place when lived in disguise in this Biraatdesa – stretched upto Kaptipada subdivision. Here the Baitarani river flows through a gorge in steps forming a series of picturesque rapids until it settles down in the pool called-Bhimkund or the Pond of Bhima .At one place the gorge is hardly four feet wide in winter; here the Baitarani disappeared underground by nature-walls giving a look of well protected pool. During Makar-sankranti , people in lakhs flock this place to take a bath in Bhimkund to wash their sins .This place has been gradually gaining importance with the celebrations of Bhimkund-mela every year which has popularized this spot as a major tourist-heritage zone, but more needs to be done to put this place in a proper tourist-maps of Eastern India.

Matsyadesa – A scholarly debate

The Fellow-scholar undertook grueling research on the various texts available regarding the exact position of

Matsyadesa as described in the Mahabharat. A number of scholars, historians, researchers have believed- few other places as Matsyadesa apart from Mayurbhanj, but all ultimately fell to the theories, places, relics, anecdotes available in this region of Mayurbhanj. The Bengali Encyclopaedia describes that – the Mahabharat famous Matsyadesa as described can be found in Rajputana of Rajasthan and also in Bombay, Mednipur in Bengal or in the hilly regions of Mayurbhanj. However the testimonial-material available only in Mayurbhanj is akin with that of Matsyadesa and it gives this region as undisputed status as Matsyadesa of Mahabharat.

Some other historians maintains that Matsyadesa might have been based at any of these places:

North Biraat state – Bharatpur in Rajasthan.

South Biraat state – Mayurbhanj region.

East Biraat state – Shahbad in Bengal.

West Biraat state – Satara in Maharastra.

However such theories that Raja Biraat of Mahabharat fame might have his empire extended & expanded up to several regions of the country is believed to be vague. But the relics available in Mayurbhanj regions only qualifies it to be the perfect Matsyadesa as described in Mahabharat ideologically, geographically, historically and from all possible angles of scholarly pursuit.

The Mahabharat maintains that, the Paandavas along with Draupadi lived one year agayaatbasa (disguised living) quite away from Hastinapur or modern Delhi which must have been situated away from it. The Paandavas were stated to hided their weapons under a big tree known as Samibrukhya which can be found only in Mayurbhanj region as its description clearly indicated that Matsyadesa was a thickly forestry region. The Mahabharat further exemplify that, Duryodhana sent several envoys to locate the Paandavas during their agayaatbasa from Indraprstha-capital of Hastinapur but none of them was able to locate them; in other words it clearly points out that, matsyadesa was situated quite a distant place from Hastinapur. The common men & clergy of matsyadesa was unable to identify Paandavas, than the most admirable persona even during their agayaatbasa. Had the matsyadesa been situated nearest to Hastinapur it could have been easier for Kaurava's to identify the Paandavas to break their agayaatbasa, which in other words clearly speaks that, matsyadesa was quite away, at a distant place from Hastinapur and was also cut off from Indraprastha politics then. In Biraat parva of Mahabharat it was stated that Judhistira the eldest of Paandavas first worshipped the presiding deity of Matsyadesa before entering in it, who was adorned with crown made up of peacocks broom as well as in its flag:

Mayurapichcha bataye keurangdadharini

Bharidebi jatha padma narayan panigraha - Biraat Parva-chapter 6, 8 sloka

Dhwajen sikhi pichchinamuchchitren birajse

Kaumaran bratamasthya tridivan pabitantwaya – Biraat Parva –chapter 6,

14 sloka

Tantra-chudamani further exemplifies that the names of the presiding deity of Matsyadesa was Ambika which is only found in Mayurbhanj region, giving credence to the only place as Matsyadesa. Even the origin of Maa Ambika place is also found in Deokund in the thickly mountaneous, forested belts of Mayurbhanj. As described in Mahabharat, here Draupadi used to made her juda (kasha/hair) in the right side of head before making visits to Rani Sudeshna as described in the 9th chapter 1-2 slokas of Biraat Parva:

Jugruhey dakshine parse mruduarit lochana

Basacha paridhayanko Krishna sumalinam mahat.

Draupadi used to bind her hair with flowers of malika, utpala, lotus & champaka which are abundantly found in the forest ponds of this region. The region have special leanings towards art, culture, music as Rajkumari Uttara had a special fascination for dance & music and Arjuna was her music teacher by bearing the name of Brihnnalla.

The Mahabharat describes that Kichaka was the mighty Senapati of Matsyadesa's Biraat Rajas and queen Sudeshna-Chitra, Rajkumar Dhananjay-Uttara,Rajkumari Uttarra and its frontier guards were known as baka & yakshya The language of matsyadesa was quite different from the prevalent languages of Hastinapur which unequivocally qualifies Mayurbhanj as Matsyadesa .Culturally & language wise the ideal positioning of Matsyadesa from Hastinapur must be above thousand miles away which it is.While disguised living the great Paandavas had identified themselves as Kanka, Ballava, Brihannalla, Granthika, Tantripala and Sairindhri. It is further contested that, when Paandavas were under a vow to keep their identities in disguise they must have resorted to these names inorder to hide their true identity whose affinity with names prevalent in this matsyadesa-Mayurbhanj region is found similar.

This region have abundant of horse & elephant population with the complete extinction of former & gradual diminishing of later. The major living of the inhabitants are from forest products collection, cow rearing, milking which one can found abundantly now also. The Mahabharat maintains that Duryodhana had attacked Matsyadesa by learning about its wealth & richness of cattles, milk and it has triggered the war against Matsyadesa through his associates like Trigartaraj Susharma & Angaraja Karna. The Biraat parva 16th chapter states that – the commander in chief of Matsyadesa, Raja Kichaka had plundered & defeated the Rajas of Anga, Banga, Kalinga and its kings were highly dissatisfied with such heroic acts of Kichaka and wanted to teach Matsyadesa a lesson, had joined this war .The craving eye of Kaurava's about the rich animal wealth in shape of high yielding cow & milk has given the impetus for this attack to Matsydesa. This further testifies that the positioning of Matsyadesa was near to Anga, Banga & Kalinga states which only the Mayurbhanj's geographical location ideally provides. During the Budhadeva's journey of Budhattva-prachar, there were only 16 states allover India viz; Anga, Magadh, Kashi, Kosala, Bajji, Malla, Banse, Kuru, Cheti, Matsya, Panchala, Surasena, Asaka, Abnti, Gandhara, Kambauj. Budhadev visited all these states except Matsyadea to propagate his teachings. In other words Matsyadesa had strong Brahmanic & Vedic culture where Budhadhdeva even dared not to interfere to propagate Budhism. It is clear & established fact that Vedic & Brahmanic culture have been deeply embedded in Matsyadesa region as one can see in the present Mayurbhanj also. Another theory links that the Matsyadesa of Mahabharat fame was situated near sea and the Bay of Bengal is situated just few kilometers away from it and also surrounded in the areas upto, Chandipur, Paradip, Dhamnagar, Digha etc,

Another literary treasure Sadananda-saudagar- pala states that after crossing Anga, Banga when one go towards Kalinga-rajya ,one encounters Biraat-rajya enroute. This describes the exact location suited to Mayurbhanj region only. From every scholastic angel it is now an established fact that-Matsyadesa's relics can only be found in today's Mayurbhanj as many existing materials points to this & here ends all the disputes that Mayurbhanj was the Matsyadesa of Mahabharat fame.

Cultural Heritage-Tangible & Intangible

The author have an opportunity to attend, interact a unique workshop organized by Indira Gandhi Rastriya Manav Sangrahalaya, Bhopal in Bhubaneswar this month where the theme was: protecting our cultural heritages. Many scholars addressed on the subject and this Fellow describes the unique cultural heritages of Mahabharatian era in the Matsyadesa of Mahabharata; today known as Mayurbhanj. He describes that there are two aspects to Cultural Heritages such as -Tangible Cultural Heritages (TCH) and Intangible Cultural Heritages (ICH).

The Tangible Cultural Heritages are consisting of: historical monuments, buildings and art objects. While Intangible Cultural Heritage has many forms : myths, legends, music, dance, crafts, technique, rituals which have passed on from one generation to another, Orally. Hence it is very important to study and document the hundreds of myths, legends, rituals, festivals, arts & crafts, communities, performing arts around & apart from the historical monuments. Because intangible cultural heritages is not only the heritage of those living in & around a monument area but also the common heritage of the human kind. So it is very important to document it in audio-visual and written formats. These Mahabharta era heritage sites & its surrounding areas have been preserving a huge number of Cultural Expressions over these years, but if left unattended, all precious heritage would be lost to oblivion and the future generation will never know its past glory, history and cultural store house. The Fellow stress on the needs of exploring further that how the Intangible elements have been contributing for development of society.

BHANJA VIGNETTE

MANAGEMENT OF HERITAGE ART CULTURAL INSTITUTIONS

SECTION: B

BHANJA VIGNETTE

Neglected Heritage sites

This Matsyadesa houses several relics, monuments, anecdotes, sites, heritage spots in its interior Similipal biosphere region which is a great tourist place dating back to Mahabharatian era,it is believed.The modernization process of this route by earmarking few crores of central grant and surrounding walls restoration is a appreciative step.

There are huge neglected heritage sites allover this Mahabhrtian era fame Matsyadesa or modern Mayurbhanj on which a vivid documentation with photographic details have been attempted.The Nrutyakothi or dance palace of kings on which a photo documentation was made used by the kings but it is found that this old heritage building of around 1800 AD has been razed to ground by administration and in its place the newly constructed district treasury building has been erected.This heritage building was in very dilapidated condition and was a den of antisocial elements,criminals as it was in an abandoned state by the ruling family, the criminals very often hide the smuggled goods such as timber and other articles. Few persons have encroached the frontage of this heritage building site and have raised jhopdi, dhaba etc for which the administration receives a number of complaints and it was razed to ground and the new district treasury building have comeup. Interestingly the district administration found it more appropriate to raze it to dust instead of salvaging its ruinous condition to its former glory as a place of tourists interests before the process of its restoration.A local orgn has since last few years trying to restore it to its architectural designs and communications with few authorities were made but this heritage building of Bhanja's is found to be disappeared from the region of Matsyadesa.

Another visiting place is Gouranga Temple situated nearby the Mayurbhanj palace which was built by Maharaja Jaganath BhanjDeo between 1600 to 1643 AD.This historic shrine has special mention in the history of Mayurbhanj as during the visit of Shri Chaitanya Mahaprabhu this temple was built to commemorate his visit to this region.

The famous Brahmo Samaj temple built with the patronization of Mayurbhanj Maharaja Sri Ramchandra

BhanjDeo who has been highly influenced by noted Brahmo Samaj founder Sri Keshab Chandra Sen of Bengal.This Brahmo temple has been rebuilt after efforts were takenup by this author in highlighting it in media.

Maharani Laxmikumari Dharmasala

The ancient heritage building of Maharani Laxmikumari Dharmasala near Sri Jaganath temple was built by Maharaja Sri Ramchandra Bhanj Deo during 1905-06 for the short stay of tourists, devotees visiting to this temple area, as this area have several deities & temples. Laxmikumari Devi is the beloved wife of Maharaja who died of malaria, than a dreaded disease & in her memory this dharmasala was built which used for free bording, lodging for short stay tourists for many years. After the merger of Mayurbhanj state the state endowment department have taken charge of its maintenance and first it imposed a tariff than increase it until 2003 when the MP Birbhadra Singh has funded this dharmasala & changed it into sadbhavana mandap by defacing, reconstructing it from behind its back, as a result it has lost its past ambience of its heritage grandeur. Today it has completely converted into a commercial centre and needs high payments for the its users. During Maharaja's time it was a practice that they built rest houses every 9 miles corresponding to 12 km distance which are today neglected, dilapidated & become the centre of all antisocial acts. Speedy takenup of reconstruction of these ancient rest houses is the need of the hour. One such covered here is Nichuapada built during the Bhanja's period.

Maa Dwarsuni Temple

One of the most ancient deity is Maa Dwarsuni believed to be appeared enroute on the ghat of national highway no 5,6.Earlier She was worshipped under a banyan tree and every passersby vehicles stop for a while to paid obeisance to Her. It is a common belief that those stop to worship Her reach their destination smoothly & safely.The deity is worshipped not by Brahmins but by non-brahmins called as Dehuri's.Today a temple has comeup in & around Maa Dwarsuni or Goddess of Doorway and become a tourists spot as seen from the photofeature.

Haripur Fort

The legendary neglected heritage site Haripur was the capital of Matsyadesa Mayurbhanj during 1400 AD after the Sultan Ferozshah Tughlaq destroyed its ancient capital in 1361 AD at Khijjing-kota or todays Khiching. Several historical sources pointed out that Haripur was the capital of Bhanja's during 1300 – 1630 AD. Few other historians are of the opinion that, it was founded by Harihara Bhanj during 1322 saka era or 1400AD. Some other historians maintains that it was founded by Harikrishna Bhanj who ruled during 1464 to 1491. Haripur or earlier Hariharapur fort is also popularly known as Bankatigada i.e,fort built after clearingup forests, which is at present in ruins and three temples – Rasikarai or Rasikaraj,Radhamohan,Sri Jaganath are found in its ruinous zone.The temple of Rasikarai today also stands with its early splendour with the Archaeological Survey of India's (ASI)effort. Most of the art & architecture depicts the influence of Vaishnavism with high degrees of Mughal era architectural style.This fact was indicated by many early researchers which has been established by this fellow-author during the study of certain architectural designs of Mughal era.Very near to this place in eastern India's Murshidabad the Namakharam Mahal (traitors palace)stands today whose designs are very much synonymous with Haripur fort & its heritage buildings. The one common factor between these structures are the rectangular shaped bricks whose thickness is about 1.5 inch but its length & breadth are about 18 & 8 inches respectively. The dome of Haripur fort today houses Rasikraj, Jaganath temples alongwith the most ruinous structures of Radhamohan temple. The ASI has actively took steps to revive the lost splendour of these two ancient temples & able to reproduced the bricks exactly in shape & size of those era and have facelifted two of the temples to a major extent to its former glory. No deities are presently there but the temples bears the testimony of the great tastes of Bhanja rulers & their love for aesthetics.The temple of Radhamohan situated within the fort zone is in dilapidated condition and no effort was taken by ASI to reinvent it. Similarly there is an underground structure equivalent with two big halls which the locals call the Cell to keep dreaded criminals. Some others are also of the view that, these were used by queens for their personal upkeep purposes. Whatever its uses were, the last excavation made by ASI during 80's in this area has also invented these two halls which also put an enigma before all. Apart from these, there are several tombs, pillars, domes, walls which silently depicts the rich cultural heritages of the erstwhile Bhanja rulers of Mayurbhanj. These several spots have either not completely excavated by ASI or remain halfdone with lack of political, historical interests & the dearth of funds.The ASI is gradually building an encompassing compound wall alongwith its main gates & other such relics carefully to reinvent the past magic of Haripur,the former capital of Bhanja's famous as Matsyadesa during the Mahabharat era. There are two big ponds near this fort zone,one of which keep water round the year -the big one but the more deep one remains always dry except few months during rainy season. Locals attributes it to the curse of Maharani for this unique phenomenon. This place was flourished to its full during Jaganath Bhanj who married to the daughter of Gajapati Raja of Puri, Shri Prataprudradeva. Once Pratrudradev was journeying for piligrimage to Brindaban via Ramchandrapur enroute Mayurbhanj and suddenly fell ill and breathed his last here. He asked his son in law to make arrangements for his 'aaradhyadeva' Shri Jaganath and accordingly the Raja made arrangements of this Jaganath temple.The village where Gajapatiraja Prataprudradeva breathed his last was renamed after him as Pratap-pur & bears the testimony of those era. The Jaganath, Balabhadra, Subhadra idols are being worshipped in the Pratappur Jaganath temple instead of Haripur fort temple, when Kalapahad attacked this region.

Sri HariBaladevjew Jagannath Temple

The major cultural & also spiritual festival of odisha is Ratha-yatra or popularly known as Car festival allover and Matsyadesa, Mayurbhanj's place comes next after Puri since tha Maharja of Mayurbhanj-the Bhanja's have donated graciously for the observance of niti-puja with grandeur. The HariBaladevjew temple otherwise known as Sri Jagannath temple is dating back to 1575 AD and built by Maharaja Shri Baidyanath BhanjDeo. A peep into its landed property invested since the times of Bhanja's with khata no,plot no,area,mauza villagewise are too vast to be documented here.However it surfaces during the course of this study that thousand acres of Haribaldevjew temple land property has been dispapppeared from the record of rights registers of the deity, questioning the vast mismanagement of temple land administration.

The issue was raised by the author and the chief minister call for a meeting to recoup the Jaganath temple land from the encroachers. The problem with the lands are: they officially belongs to Jaganath temple to be enjoyed by its sevayats but with each passing years the new generations have devised ways & means to record it in their personal names striking the names of Lord Jaganath,which has created a number of conflicts,litigations as well as disruptions in the niti-puja of Lord Jaganath.Perhaps allover the country people donate to God but except very few,in this land of odisha many found to be record the properties of temple in their own names.Similarly the issues of ornaments given by the Maharajas of Mayurbhanj to the temple has also found to be disappeared from its treasury causing much furore in the media which has also been takenup specially by this author.

Heritage Air fields

The heritage air fields evolved, developed during erstwhile kings of certain feudatory states which now comes under newly curvedout districts. One such famous is Amarda Air strip or field developed by Britishers during IInd world war 1939-1945. This air field is presently located in the exstate of Mayurbhanj under Rasgobindpur block.Hundreds of acres were donatedby former Maharaja on which facilities for landing of eight airplanes at a time have been developed.Its runways have eight such pads on which airplanes engaged in IInd world war came to took rest here. The airbase has many undergrounds, pillars, walls, rest shades out of which severals have been razed to ground by encroachers in absence of proper maintenance. Hundreds of acres of its lands though found to be record ed in govt but possessed by outsiders as such little protection was meted to this heritage site as a result the area has been encroached by many and since 2004 construction of palatial buildings by few have surfaced in this protected zone.It is the only airstrip available to eastern India under the Chandipur DRDO & Kaleikunda airbase and used as a base for landing dignatiries like President,Pimeminister etc.The other heritage air bases are at Rajaloka, Fatehgarh, Jharsuguda, Barbil, Dandbose-to name a few in the entire state apart from Bhubaneswar aerodrum.

Jubilee Library

Another heritage site is Jubilee Library-a name given by Maharaja Sri Ramchandra BhanjDeo which commensurates the jubilee year of the Empress Queen Victoria, London & designed in unique British style.The Maharja initially setup a library (pathagara) in his royal palace & in 1893-94 he expands it to the Jubilee library and also the founder President till his last. The Maharaja has formed an autonomous committee to manage its affairs which is still continuing.This heritage building is also known as Sri Ramchandra Pathagara since 1901. Now its entire area is surrounded with boundaries and has possessed rare books, journals in its collections.Lateron the management of this pathagara has been taken up by culture department, govt. of odisha.

Lulung & Sitakund

Another heritage as well as tourist site is Lulung & Sitakund- a perennial stream exists & attracts thousands of tourists ,also the entry point of Similipal sanctuary.It also houses many Mahabharatian era site,relics and now the department of tourism have a tourist bunglow here for the stay of visitors round the year.

Raghunathjew Shrine

There are two famous heritage shrines Raghunaathjew-one at Jahipur and another at Baripada.The regular theft of ornaments given by Bhanja rulers and embezzlement of landed properties of the Jews donated by Maharaja's as niti-puja today are facing major crisis which needs to be replaced with more vigilant approach as well as dedicated sevayats.

Nagra-bhadi or Nagada House

Nagra-bhadi or Nagada house, a particular instrument with a roaric sound is an old heritage building situated infront of the famous Jaganath Temple of Baripada built during 1575 AD by Maharaja's of Mayurbhanj.It contains a thrre storied layers of nagda players in this mansion when the Lord Jaganath's morning, noon & evening aarti begans.The tradition of nagra worshipping continued till seventies and during eighties it was on the wane. This famous tradition of nagra and their players came to a close in absence of patronization and today this heritage building has been encompassed with several encroachments as number of shops have denigrated its monumental value.Thus families ekingout their living out of this nagra-playing tradition are a vanished lot.

Bhudhara- Chandi Heritage temple

The Nilgiri fort range has a unique temple heritage site of Maa Bhudhara-Chandistated to be appeared from the earth itself during 15th century under a neem tree. As the deity had appeared from under the earth She is named Bhudhara. The temple depicts around 106 images of different deities depicting from Mahabharat era. It was built during 1905 by the Nilgiri Raja ShyamSunder

Mardaraj.It is one of the major neglected but famous Shakti-pithain northern odisha in most dilapidated consition and needs immediate patronization.

Bhanja's worshipper of Bishnu cult

A 15th century dilapidated Bishnu temple came to limelight in the village Padmapur-Deuli in Jharpokharia area which speaks the Bhanja's devotion towards Bishnu-Narayana. Infact if one goes through the geneology of Bhanja dynasty one would found that some of the Bhanja's were Shaivites, some Vaishnavites & some belongs to Jaganath cult, whereas some, Chaitanyaties-followers of Shri Chaitanyadev Mahaprabhu. Such cult worshipped configured the royalty for certain period at a certain time.The said Bishnu idols recovered from the underneath, is about 3 feet 10 inch which epitomized the four arms-chaturbhuja posture of the deity with sankh, chankra, gada, padma. Noted researchers of this area are of the view that, the name of the village Padmapur-Deuli probably stems from this Bishnu idol. The village is surrounded with six Brahmin- sasans which confirms the worship in the Bishnu temple.

Mayurbhanj Textiles

Mayurbhanj Textile Mill setup By Durbar Administration during Bhanja's in this underdeveloped backward region which started production in 1943 with the installation of imported machineries from England and was a profit making factory until the merger of Mayurbhanj .Thereafter its shares & stakes were transferred to govt of odisha which manged its affairs till 1960. But the state govt.mananged public limited company with an authorized share capital of 6 lakh and paidup capital of 2.50 lakh, it has 62% of the share. Its finished products on hosiery items have wide local as well as national markets outside odisha & especially in kolkata, Mumbai. But the state govt appointed boards mismanagement has put this heritage factory into a grinding halt from 1962. In 1992 the then chiefminister Biju Patnaik gave 10 lakh package for its revival but there was lockup in the factory due to mismanagement.All the trainees mostly tribals lost their skills, many have lost their jobs and the factory's 109 acres of valuble land adjacent to it attached by Bhanja rulers during 40's become bone of contention for the future royalty of the dynasty. The brother of Bhanja kings having two wives one is from Bastar state & another from this locality having different stakes on this property and thus a legal court battle was ensued between them. However taking advantage of long years of absence of Maharani of Bastar the local descendants have started selling the valuable 109 acres of Textiles land to different persons since 1979.As a result the area encompassing this textiles has been completely disappeared and only its boundary walls have been enveloped from all sides to this heritage zone. This entire heritage zone today is found to be completely overshadowed by private houses, sold illegally by one of the descendants of Lalsaheb Prafulla Chandra BhanjDeo .Thus the entire heritage Textiles buildings, lands, machineries have all sold to different parties and except this boundary walls nothing is available on the site.

Belgadia Palace

The palace of Bhanja rulers situated in the middle of Baripada town sprawling across 25 acres of land situated amidst thick greenary. The present day population have seen the rise & fall of many rulers starting from Sri Ramchandra BhanjDeo to Purna Chandra Bhanj, Pratap

Chandra Bhanj, Pradip Chandra Bhanj and now Pravin Chandra BhanjDeo, who usually stays at Kolkata but often came to this ancient palace, the glory of Bhanjas. The palace is managed by a team of staffs which put a bar on taking snaps of this palace without permission of royalty. The Fellow thus undertook only the photos of entrance royal gate of this palace along with the stonewalls built around this famous Belgadia palace – a heritage site of Bhanjas and prefers to wait for the royalty to arrive from Kolkata when the necessary permission to photo-document the palace would be made in detail.

Budha-Raula Mahadev Matha

Another heritage dimension of art & culture is Budha-raula Mahadev. The Mahadev was appeared after a sadhu sat here on 'dhuni' for years in the river bank of chipat. Locals here call the Mahadev as Budha-raula.This is a famous Shiva temple as well as Matha which has been renovated with ministers local area development fund of 5 lakh way back to 2002. A dhuni-ashram site, temple, storage and main temple was renovated by few local enthusiast on this Bhanja rulers heritage buildings.

Mayurbhanj Palace: A site of Royal heritage

The Bhanjas were lover of grandeur and style and it is said that the Mayurbhanj Palace built by Sri Ramchandra Bhanj was designed on the line of Britains Buckingham Palace. This royal palace was one of the best testimony of Bhanja royalty as it sprawls across few acres having dome, structures and swimming pools, temples everything. The Durbar Hall was one of the magnificient arena where royalty of different states used to gather during important occasions like famous Mayurbhanj Chhau festival, Makarsankranthi or any other festivities when the real grandeur of royalty speaks to people. This palace was donated by Maharaja Purna Chandra Bhanj during 50's for opening of a College in his name which still bear it today by giving access to common men to know about the royalty of Bhanjas. The durbar halls have been converted into classrooms, the Maharani swimming pool has been redesigned as library of the college and many such changes have been embedded in its walls & structures. However this bears a unique testimony to the Bhanja heritage.

Makar-sankranti mela- A unique heritage rites of local tribes

The famous Makarsankranti mela is observed allover Mayurbhanj which since the State-period to till date is a major state festival. The local tribals like santhals, bathudi, bhumij came to river Balanga to exoncrate their dead men's bone on the river, a festival which continue for a week. Similar Makar festival was celebrated at Samibrukhya as described earlier and it was also witnessed many local cultural teams, unique to this region.

Talsari – Tourism zone in need of patronage

This tourist spot is situated bordering Digha, having unraveled famous spots such as, Bhusandeswar Shiva, Chandeneswar, Basuli, Astasambhu of Dahmunda, Baradeuli, Jaganath temple of Kamarda, a tourism growth plan of 80 crore since long is pending due to political rampage. Half a dozen politicians have assured many things so far but this unique heritage tourist zone in Bhograi-Talsari sea beach is still languishing amidst wanton funds & patronage. A peep into this unique zone.

Creamation-Places or Personal Holdings

An alarming trend noted by the scholars that creamation-ghats are fast encroached by persons, builders in collaboration with govt. officials into converting dwelling places illegally. Several such crematorium- ghats locally known as Shamsans are being encroached fast by several illegal occupants .This has shrinked the serenity in the cremation area and increased the pollution & other hazards. Samsan-ghats are even not free for departed souls which is a major trauma of modern times. The scholar-fellow also given his initiatives of 2001 while protesting such acts by few of a particular community and also how he was treated by causing injury & harm while working for this common interest.

Deokund – A major shakti-pitha

There are 51 shakti-pitha allover and the famous ones are: Jwalamukhi in Kangra valley of Himachal Padesh where the 'tongue'of Mata Shakti was fallen.Katyani' in Brindaban,where the 'hair' was fallen.Kanyakumari,where the 'shoulder & back of mata' was fallen and 'Kamakhya'mandir in Guwahati of Assam where 'Shakti's 'yoni' was fallen.These four pitha's are major shaktipitha's alongwith 47 other places where the pieces of Mata Shakti was stated to be fallen after She was torn into pieces by an angry Shiva-Her husband. Deokund is another place in this matsyadesa region where part of the 'yoni' of Mata was believed to be fallen and it is the origin place of Maa Ambika-as shakti is known here. The Brahmin told that before the rajasankranti – a major festival in odisha during the month of June. The temple which is situated amidst the sylvan surroundings of Similipal's region and much above the land level on a rocky mountaneous range, with a high power current water fall, the temple closes for four days,as the water is found to be "red' during these days.In other words it is a 'rajaswala' period of "Mata or yearly cycle of period. During these days all sorts of worship in this pitha is stopped. The place is an ideal spiritual place where tourists and devotees flock together in large numbers.A two hour drive from headquarter Baripada, this place is now having good motorable roads courtesy PMGSY and lot of improvements in road infrastructure has been developed. One needs to ascend around hundreds of stairs builtup on rocky stones to reach this pitha where Maa Ambika is believed to be originated. A mysterious atmosphere along with mythical surroundings has given rise to many folklore and exudes a rare spiritual mystical charm here where once Lalsaheb Prafulla chandra BhanjDeo ,the brother of king used to come & practise his 'tantra'sadhana,wrote Devi tantra Sadhana, extensively.

Maharaja Shri Ramchandra Jayanti politicized

The Maharaja Sri Ramchandra BhanjDeo's birthday 17 Dec was observed by the admn.& people alike every year,but the ugly politicization of Jharkhand leders have put a bandh call on this very day which resulted allover unrest on some flimsy grounds.Intellectuals of the region have criticized the jharkhandi's for their such acts detrimental to regional interests.Number of incidents reported from allover due to this unrest.A number of political leders alongwith some local mediamen have degenerated this auspicious birthday of Maharaja into a political gimmick.

Similarly the scion of Maharaja Sri Pravin Chandra BhanjDeo alongwith Rajmata Bharati Rajlaxmi Devi was misbehaved by a MVI in Laxmannath checkgate-the border in odisha-Bengal when despite the Maharaja's identifiction statement, the officials said- I donot know any Maharaja,I am the Maharaja of this place'.This led to serious administrative & public debate about the discourteous behaviour of certain employees who are so eager to earn bribe that in their lust they even unable to recognize man of royalty.This surely is a fall in virtues & display decay in our culture.

Kamardiha Matha-A ruinous heritage site

The Maharajas of Mayurbhanj were fond of establishing Matha-temple cum-rest sheds during their tenure and many such matha's are fast disappearing with the modern hotel-culture'.Khunta-Kamardiha matha situated in Rasgobindpur block is one such neglected heritage site.Its massive landed property situated at Baunsatofa, kamardiha, khunta, panchmania, jharia, Majnadiha, Dhansole,Bhandabhati are now illegally captured & even recorded officially this was disclosed during the field-study of the scholar.A number of temple-matha management officials are involved in such illegal transfer of deity's landed property which has been unearthed during this visit.A number of locals have demaned the restoration of deity's property in the name of khunta-kamardiha matha as before.The matha,it is said that, the biggest royt in this entire region whose cultivation & yielding of crops runs to lakhs every year.However the rampant irregularities have deprived the matha & its deity as well as dependants tenants,the accrued benefits by the scholar along with photographic details of -a rare heritage site since long.

Kakharua Baidyanath: Cultural heritage of Bhanja Dynasty

The study of one of the most ancient heritage site, divine institution believed to be directly blessed by Lord Kakharua Baidyanath, incarnation of Lord Shiva.

According to popular prevalent folklores of this region there are a number of anecdotes associated with this traditional cultural heritage institution which become instrumental in setting up of this rich divine, tourists & worship spot. This famous heritage spot is in Manatri,36 km from the headquarter of Mayurbhanj and is situated on the river Gangahaar. Once the Puri-Gajapati Raja was suffering from deadly leprosy disease and during his pilgrimage and sojourn near this site, he was instructed by Lord in his dreams that Lord Shiva is under the pumpkin (kakharu, locally known) tree and he digged it and found Shiva linga inside the river Gangahaar and started worshipping. During heavy rainy days, the shiva-linga was inundated with flood waters; showing this, the pujak fall prostrated and since that year, the river turn its course, leaving a trail of water streams known as kundi on which this cultural heritage site has been erected. The most significant part of this heritage site is, all the Shiva-lingams allover are worshipped by bel-patta; here Kakharua Baidyanath Shiva is being worshipped with both tulsi & bel leaves. As it was appeared beneath a kakharu leaf tree, it is popularly known as such.

According to another popular folklore, once a cowherd boy was guarding the cows and found one of its milchcow is not in the group. He made frantic search of this cow and found it in the bank of river Gangahaar where it was standing near a kakharu leaf tree and milk was pouring from its body. The next day he also found that this partcular cow is regularly going to that particular spot and sprinkling milk underneath this kakharu tree. He narrated this entire incident to villagers who came and digged the place and found Shiva linga, which later on led for establishments of today's famous Kakharua Baidyanath Pitha. A nuimber of villagers had donated each three maan (around a bigha) of land for this pitha for which this area is known as Manatri meaning three- mana and lateron Bhanja Kings were instrumental for constructing this heritage site structure.

This heritage-cultural temple was probably built during later 14th & early 15th century AD according to few other scholar- historians, when the famous Puri Gajapati Raja Kakharua Dev and in Mayurbhanj Maharaja Balabhadra BhanjDeo was ruling this region. During the visit of Puri-Gajapati the construction of this temple might have begun. Another mythology holds that during 1556 AD it was built by Mahaaja Baidyanath BhanjDeo who was also the builder of famous Shri Hari Baladev jew(Jaganath) temple in Baripada. The fact is historically verifiable as the structures, domes, natamandir of Kakharua pitha are largely identical with this Jagannath temple and it is quite different from usual shiva temples. He established the idols of Lord Jagannath in this pitha hence an ideal place of worship for Hari (Vishnu) & Hara (Shiva). Everyday the temple includes a kakharu as its prasaad and despite a shiva-pitha it usually observes all the festivals of Jagannath temple with equal fervour & grandeur like ratha-yatra, devasnan, jhulan, dolapurnima. But the most important & unique festival here is Maha Shivaratri which usually observed for a fortnight every year with lakhs of devotees thronging from allover. This rich heritage site & temple have hundreds of acres of land engaged by Bhanja rulers for the smooth management of deity & temple with grandeur. Baba Kakharua Baidyanath is surrounded with Shri Loknath, Shri Maliknath, Shri Kundanath, Shri

Barahnath, Shri Swapneswarnath apart from Mahveer-Hanuman, Maa Durga.

Its raw flavour during Maha Shivaratri and the most scenic part is the appearance of deity from the river bed. A number of photo-essays on this site is given herewith exclusively to depict the unique heritageness of this place.

Manatri & Kuradiha Garh

In this region two famous garhs, forts viz, Manatrigarh, Kuradihagarh and Mangobindpur-garh were stated to be existed. Once Manatrigarh was existed near Manatri village stated to be built during Maharaja ShriDam Chandra BhanjDeo which once was a flourishing area. Mangobindpur garh was stated to be established by Gajapati Kakharua Raja's dewan- Gobinda Bidyadhara who after killing the former had captured this fort. The remains of both these garhs, heritage sites are hardly available today except their wall-edges at one or two places which simply reminds one of their ancient importance. Similarly kuradihagarh is situated enroute to Manatri-Baripada which today has converted into a rest house with few addition & alteration. This fort has four big halls and the Bhanja kings were stated to play dice in this place. Maharaja Damodara BhanjDeo took shelter during Marhattas invasion which the later have desecrated and made a heap of bricks in village kuradiha.

Baruneswar Mahadev

This famous site is situated in a spring called Baruni and known as such. This place of worship was built by Lalsaheb Prafulla Chandra BhanjDeo, the younger brother of Mmaharaja who was engaged himself with number of occultism, tantra etc and used to meditate most of the time in this serene place. Lord Baruneswara Mahadev is the presiding deity to this gateway to heavens; as the famous Hindu cremation place known as Barunighat exist just by its side, which was setup during Maharaja Shri Ramchandra BhanjDeo and later on renovated for the use of humanity since then.

Sarada Mandir : abode of Lalsaheb's

The Sarada-mandir is one of the heritage temple situated in the precincts of Lalsahebs – the king's brothers. It was treated as a personal temple of Lalsahebs till merger and after it was opened for general public. Maharaja's built several temples –many for personal worshipping & few for public entry & worshipping. Jwalamukhi, Purnachandra, Maa Kichakeswari - all were built around the protected premises of Maharaja's which after the kingship, was opened for public wroshipping. Maa Sarada temple is the personal temple of Lalsaheb Nirmal Chandra BhanjDeo family who carry all its responsibilities-from maintenance to establishment. The area of Maa Sarada temple is later on built with a hotel- Grand, Kichaka, a cinemahall - Roxy and a cycle stand. The income from these establishment go for the development & niti-puja of Sarada temple. Navaratri is being celebrated here with gaiety. Its adjacent areas are covered with shop rooms and its periphery management is important with regard to its heritageness.

Saras-kshetra of Lord Jaganath

Lord Jaganath is the deity allover people worship and number of temples were constructed apart from Puri & Baripada and one such is Lord Jaganath of Saraskshetra, situated at Saraskona. Around 40 km from district headquarter Baripada, Saraskona is situated bordering Bengal & Jharkhand and became a constant headache for administration with regard to maoist & Naxalites infiltration over these years. Bad road condition alongwith local groupism mindsets has put this Saraskshetra - Saraskona as one of the most law & order troubled area in Mayurbhanj. Recently the delimitation commission has declared Saraskona as a separate assembly constituency & for the first time it is being represented in assembly and people hope for its overall development. Saraskshetra-Saraskona have revived this Jaganath temple in 2002 with the active involvement of Puri Gajapatiraja and the temple is now built with modern styles .Its adjacent haat gives royalty from its income to the temple & the collection from temple-hundi.. The area is completely neglected & its revival with Jaganath culture has put some sort of religiosity with regard to the lawless elements, disturbing peace in this area.

Chahla-Heritage tourist site in rampage

The Maharaja's of Mayurbhanj were lovers of nature, hunting & Similipal plateau provides them with an ideal site of thick forest amidst natural beauty. The Maharaja's have built Chahala Forest rest House (FRH) where during winter months, they used to come for rest, relaxation & hunting .With years passby several FRH were also built by them at scenic locations like – Nwana, Gudgudia, Barhakamuda, where forest beat house alongwith these luxury rest houses were built by them. Lateron used by tourists on payment. The Chahala FRH- the most oldest heritage house was ransacked recently by hooligans threatening tourists not to invade their abode. They had damaged part & parcel of this heritage house which the media termed as acts of maoist. Whatever the menace is - this heritage house was disfigured due to such rampage whose upgradation into former royal status is found to be a difficult job.

Astamprahari-baadi-pala culture –on wane

The region interlinked with Bengal, Jharkhand has also express its unique culture of baadi-paala & astam-prahari. In baadi-paala the villagers contributed cash, rice and young girls recite literary creations of Madhusudan Roy, Radhanath Ray, Fakirmohan's poem (kaavya) & also Bhagavata, Mahabharata. In astam-prahari culture, a troupe of kirtaan singers used to play khol, kirtaan in a turnaround way by installing Narayan. This round about ways of reciting God's glory for days together without any breaks in between, is said to be a gift of Mahaprabhu Shri Chaitanyadev's culture. Shri Chaitanyadev of Goudia matha in Bengal have highly mesmerized people in this region and round the year- be it chaitra or baisakha purnima till the end of Raas-purnima- this is evident allover, round the year. The peculiar character of this culture is –whatever the condition or situation is, be it flood, drought or rain, winter it has always propelled people in the tribal villages also to prepare such cultural fiesta off & on to remind the glory of great ancient heritage once this region bears. This culture of late although threatened by the invasion of new entertainment culture of cinema, TV has again revived in most gigantic manner by the simple villages folk and largely attributed to them.

Matsyadesa-Mayurbhanj: A Cultural Fiesta

The contiguous culture of Mahabharat fame Matsyadesa-today's Mayurbhanj is the birth place of many cultures, traditions & languages. The Santhali language took birth on the soil of Mayurbhanj & its propounder Pandit Raghunath Murmu. The renaissance in education was caused by Ravenshaw College established at Cuttack; so also the SriRamchandra Bhanj Medical college- these were the early landmark to augment new vistas in development by the Maharaja's of Mayurbhanj. Enlightened, highly educated, the benevolent kingship of Bhanja rulers in this Mahabharat fame Matsyadesa is a landmark in every direction. Maharaja's of Mayurbhanj had extend massive funds support for compilation of Oriya Bhashakosh- which was named as Purnachandra Oriya Bhashakosh in eight parts and is considered a treasure of Oriya language. The Bhanja rulers had donated around 8 lakh to Utkal University when it was first setup in 1951 & for the first time students of Orissa were freed from the administrative control of Patna University, as earlier it was administered from Bihar. Manorma & Utkalprava, Mayurbhanj chronicle, Bhanja-Pradip were few cultural-linguo journals published, promoted by Bhanja rulers which had featured almost all the literary doyens of that times and are considered today as rich treasure of culture, language & heritage. The ingredients of culture & rich heritageness was so deeply embedded that this soil later on produced many films-actors, producers, singers, directors, cinematographer and also provides panoramic view for film shooting till eighties. After this, the divisive politics has engulfed this region & its rich cultural heritage is stated to be encroached, crushed to the debris of shortlived consumerism .But as historians say- its cultural dimension is so vast that, time & trends may pass on it but unable to crush this century old Mahabharatian-Matsyadesa region- Mayurbhanj into dust. It's sublime heritageness is eluding the minds of future generations to witness.

Mahabharatian Heritage : Kichakeswari Temple

The many sites dating back to Mahabharatian era as the local myths & tales depict the site and events, Raja Kichaka, the brother–in-law of famous Viraat-Raja of Mahabharata fame had his capital at Khijingkota, as known to historians and today it is famous as Khiching and its presiding deity called Kichakeswari. It was believed that Kichakeswari was the presiding deity of Bhanja kings and in a number of places the idols of Maa Kichakeswari was found. In the Mayurbhanj palace itself, the western gate of the palace was the entry point of Maa Kichakeswari and it was closely worshipped by Bhanja kings exclusively by them only and outsiders were not allowed inside the temple. It is said that the temple Goddess was very effective (pratakhya)to the prayers of kings who inturn worship Her everyday and on some special occasions like, leading the armed forces on victory mission. The temple during the occasion of dussehra had witnessed large number of animal sacrifice including buffalo in its precincts which the royalty was fond of, to appease the deity. This palace temple was first opened to general public by Maharaja Pratap Chandra BhanjDeo during late 60's.Thereafter it was opened for all the time. The morning & evening worship bell of the temple reverberetes the whole palace precincts which several students used to witnessed as the palace was turned into a college by the Maharaja Purnachandra BhanjDeo. The temple has entry door like the Mughal era sculpture and its nata-mandap is like Hindu temple. The place where animals were sacrificed on tying on their heads has still withstood the time, engraving the blood of animal sacrifice, a saga of royalty.

The Kichakeswari Devi is the presiding deity of Bhanja kings till date and after the merger of Mayurbhanj state in

1949,its precincts was gradually diminished of celebrations like nitipuja, animal sacrifice etc for a longtime for dire want of funds and absence of royal patronage. But the present Maharaja Praveen Chandra BhanjDeo took a special interest in bringing back its past glory and accordingly reconstruction work begun and it has restored to its former glory. Now it performs its nitipuja and is open for public all the time. A number of photographs of this unique Mahabharatian era temple.

Jajneswara Mahadev Temple

The Maharaja Shri Ramchandra BhanjDeo had donated vast acres of land to his mentor & guru, the noted Sanskrit scholar Sri Gobinda Chandra Mohapatra who took the reins of administration while tutoring the adolescent Maharaja. In conform to guru-dakshina the Maharaja gave away lands on which Sri Mohapatra, the eminent author of translating Mahabharat in Sanskrit which later got sahitya akademi award had constructed a Shiva temple known as Jajneswar Temple in early 1900s. His own mortal body was engulfed to flame in this temple precincts. After the demise of Pandit Mohapatra his ancestors form a trust to look after this temple which was then outskirts of the town area, but with changing times it is now in the midst of crowded area. Later on the trustees have adjoined a Maa Durga temple to this main Shiva temple. Few photo documents to enliven the importance of this temple.

Benu Madhab Math : Paandava's place of worship

The study of Mahabharatian era Matsyadesa with greater depths and connected the rich, resplendent region of nature from many historians, researchers of past who has some or other way worked in this region, on subjects other than this. The famous such persons were Nilamani

Senapati, S.N. Sarkar, J.K. Sahu, Dr K.C. Panigrahi, Dr H.K. Mahatab, Janmejay Sahu, P.K. Dash to name a few who have depicted the place & region in their writings as a natures gift to world, but many have unable to draw such similarities of Mahabharatian era relics, except in an sporadic manner. As stated earlier the area in Raruan where Sahadeva & Nakula were looking after the cow-cattles of Raja Biraaat is a fertile land where crops grow immensely and the people were fond of eking out their living out of cattle rearing & grazing. Apart from a little distance of Biraat fort in Khiching comes the natures paradise, Similipal sanctuary. The Panch Paandavas were stated to be accompanying Raja Biraat during his 'mrigayaa' or hunting spree to this region. The Pandava's along with Sairindri or Draupadi were also accompanying Raja Biraat & his queen Sudeshna during their hunting and legend established that there is a BeniMadhb math-temple in this deep, dense forest zone and which probably they were worshipping. Because under what circumstances a Krishna or BeniMadhab temple was constructed by whom, & when is still an enigma. As the Paandavas were the sakha's and the worshipper of Lord Krishna, they have devoted their stay in worshipping HIM in this thick forest secretly. The area now is under reserve forest division of Similipal Authority. The Fellow also consulted with some elders about this and they had also substantiated this view that, when there is no population movement nor it falls on the usual human habitat route this might have built by the Paandavas. The Fellow covered few other Bhanja heritage sites with greater depth.

Surya Nivas-Modern Management Institute

This heritage building was built since the days of Maharaja Pratap Chandra BhanjDeo and popularly known as Surya Nivas- or Sun House. The name does not indicate any special significance except that it is situated just few yards from famous Brahmo temple. Maharaja Sri Ramchandra BhanjDeo was an astute believers of Brahmo doctrines since the days of his schooling at Darjeeling & even fallen in love with famous Brahmo leader Keshab Chandra Sen's daughter. It was a different saga that this love couldn't materialize into marriage and the Maharaja setup Brahmo temple and there after Surya Nivas. The history of this heritage building states that, it was used for royal purpose and after the merger it has housed the Samabaya Parichalana Pratisthana or the Cooperative Management Institute to impart knowledge to strengthen the ongoing cooperative activities of the Govt. in this region. Therafter during 80's the then district administration has setup a Competitive & Career Training Centre behind its backyard rooms which continued so long the patronizer-officers were present in this area. But once they left the area, the training center was caught between groupism and affairs went into such a pass that the center was closed forever. However a local career orgn. JSP once proceeded with govt. to reopen this center but the elected representatives became a bar in its re opening .It was now clear that the elected representatives were not in favour of seeing the area's youth to be more & better qualified or successful in various competitive examinations as all the efforts were silenced. Now Surya Nivas only houses the cooperative management center in its front portion of heritage building and many years of neglect has threatened its ancient walls, floorings etc. The Fellow took few photographs of this heritage building.

HighCourt-Mayurbhanj

The benevolent Bhanja rulers knew that, their subjects were specially tribals & other economically poor who could not afford to move Highcourt then situated at Patna for justice. During 1947-57 the state comes under the jurisdiction of Patna High court & later on to Odisha Highcourt situated at Cattak. But the Maharaja's of Mayurbhanj fully realized the cost effectiveness in proceeding to higher courts, have setup a Highcourt in Mayurbhanj itself, during the royalty of Maharaja Sir Pratap Chandra BhanjDeo. Maharaja's such efforts were very much advanced of his times, maintains many historians. But after merger the govt. of Odisha ask the Maharaja to wihdraw this Highcourt as it merged under Odisha state & would have the same Highcourt jurisdiction of the state and cannot have another Highcourt. The Maharaja was agreed but urged the govt. to consider for setting a circuit bench of Odisha Highcourt in any future date, as his subjects were very much poor. Sixtyone years after also this merger provision was not acted on by the successive govt.'s in odisha which has resulted in regular strikes, bandhs on the demand of setting up a circuit court bench of Highcourt. Today the Mayurbhanj Highcourt building was used as the District Judges court. This heritage building has structures resembled with London's Buckingham Palace. Infact, the Maharaja's of Mayurbhanj were regular visitors to British royalty & had been greatly influenced by their style, domes and designs which reflected in several heritage buildings constructed by them.

Durbar Administrtion : Mayurbhanj State Bank

The Bhanja's were much advanced and ahead of their times in terms of ideas and building Institutions. They have built Mayurbhanj State Bank during the time of Maharaja Sir Pratap Chndra BhanjDeo which used as a royal-public treasury of funds. Interestingly many Maharja's like Bikaner, Saurashtra, Mysore, Hyderabad have setup their own State Banks, so also the Maharaja of Mayurbhanj. After independence ,the names of State Bank of Mysore, Bikaner, Rajasthan was remained intact ,but the gullible administrator have cleansed the word of Mayurbhanj in their bank and today it is simply known as State Bank of India. This ancient royal state bank is today used as a part of the local administration & revenue office works from this place. The entire Durbar administration has become completely taken over by the govt. of odisha and now collector Dist. Magistrate sits in this durbar administration hall. But the grandeur marble statue of Maharja Sri Ramchandra BhanjDeo was unveiled years back as a tribute to his special benevolence which was garlanded every year on Dec.17, his anniversary day. The atmosphere of this heritage building is equivalent with the British royalty. Its sculptures, paintings and stairs all have reminded the once vast saga of royalty in this corridor of power. A bygone era splendour coupled with mystic royalty silence greets every visitor, whosoever crosses its corridors. The Fellow undertook a photo journey on this heritage building complex.

Localself Governance-Municipality Baripada

Maharaja Sri Ramchandra BhanjDeo inorder to provide his subjects good local administration has setup the Baripada Municipality in 1905 in this heritage royalty building which completes its centenary in 2005. It was beyond the thought of his time as many of his contemporary Maharaja's, rulers were even not organized their central administration or rules; the Maharaja's of Mayurbhanj could visualize the concept of local self govt. to better the civic life. Sanitation, road, streetlighting, burning ghats etc were the main activities of this municipality then, which today has expanded with the passage of time. Utkalmani Gopabandhu Dash, the noted freedom fighter, doyen, literature was once the Vice-chairperson of this municipality and served under Bhanja kings once, which was greatly benefited from his wisdom. This ancient heritage royal building was additioned with a new building during 2005; but the grandeur, aestheticness of the Paura-Parishad building & its inner council halls are a matter of visual treat which is situated just infront of Durbar administration complex or in today's official area. The former Durbar Administration Hall is used now as Collector's office and few views were taken to chronicle the glory, the grandeur of this heritage buildings established by Bhanja's.

Maa Jwalamukhi Mandir

Jwalamukhi considered as a royal deity exclusively here and a temple in the serene atmosphere of lake was built by Lalsaheb Pramod Chandra BhanjDeo, the younger brother of Maharaja which The Goddes today exclusively maintained & manged by Lalsaheb's family. This heritage temple goddess is in pure gold and its temple top is also covered with gold. The royal family members exclusively worship the deity and common public are allowed entry at specific time of the day and not always. The Lalsaheb's also promote a film production company in this name of

Maa Jwalamukhi Films. The scholar-Fellow continue his study to several other historical places associated or believed to be habitated by Paandavas whose detail glimpse shall be provided in next report. The Fellow expresses his sincere gratitude for this unique scholarly study ever taken by anyone in this region through your kind Support.

Benisagar – The Mythical Place of Paanchali

The mythical place during Mahabharatian era-matsyadesa-Benisagar is a place to exude serenity & holiness in its environment.The place was very much a part of Mayurbhanj – then Matsyadesa until its merger in 1949 when some of its major regions were curved out to merge in odisha & few important places like Raibania, Olmara, Chinchda, Fenko including this Benisagar merged with Bihar & lateron in Jharkhand. A journey of five minutes from Mayurbhanj's Raruan block, one comes across through the signpost –Majhgaon block in West Singhbhum district in Jharkhand. A five minutes journey can take one to this most holiest places since Mahabharatian era. Benisagar as the name signifies a big pond, reservoir or lake even compared to a small dam situated amidst deep forest, cool breeze and out of noise pollution even that of a village. It was believed & ascertained by few historians that Paanchali during Paandava's agayatabasa' here was the royal accomplice of queen Sudeshna, of Raja Biraat and especially this place was used for bathing purpose of royalty. The queen along with her group of beauty maidens & Paanchali used to took bath in this water reservoir, away from commonmen's sight.It was once during her bath that Draupadi lost her 'beni"(hair) in this lake hence this name-Benisagar. The lake situated in a sylvan surroundings even today, quite away from public gaze. The entire area is covered with tall Sal trees, the hallmark of Mayurbhanj forests,where one could find a big dam like facilities have been erected. Just infront of this water pond one found the excavations of a big fort is in the process since last three years.The excavated materials include stonewares, idols builtup of black-mugni stones akin to the stone crafts of khiching. A number of Shivalingas are also found in this excavations for which it led to believe that, perhaps after secretely taking bath, the queensfolk used to worship Shiva in this temple.The excavations is in progress presently by ASI,Ranchi circle and a number of idols have been recovered in this region. But sadly the area once habitated in Mayurbhanj is now in Jharkhand. The Fellow – asked about it and got the reply that,it was very much a part of Jharkhand.Hence the forthcoming generations might never believe that it was once a part of matsyadesa –due to this political & administrative divisions, leading towards cultural bifurcation.A big museum of ASI is also under construction process and house all those excavated rare ancient materials, recovered during these digging.The quality of bricks used in these excavated fort-temple is similar to that of Haripur & Khiching –rectangular in shape but thickness is less than todays bricks.The scholar-fellow took few snaps of this place ideal for meditation as tranquility rules here but was prevented by the ASI staffs, not to photographed as it is in progress.However three photographs was already taken which are given herewith.

Keshna – Abode of Krishna'

Draupadi whose other name is Krishna was assigned this village situated just four km.from famous khiching temple after one crosses Ghikhali village on the roadside.Both the side of road one could witness a number of stoneware artisans are busy in ripping the black mugni stones and out of it, they used to design various eyecatching stonecrafts- idols of different kinds, animals other household useable items are being forked out from these stones. Around 200 craftsman lives in this area alone of which 300 are households. Almost all the major adults are being trained to become a craftsman of stone artistry, but with days passed however their number started receding as new generes are opting jobs outside this traditional mode of earning. The villagers believed that their village keshna have a never ending supply of black-mugni stone out of which they used to earn their livelihood since generations. This black mugni stone is widely used in construction of famous khiching temple once. The villagers are proud of their crafts and is lamenting on the resource crunch in this stone arts & crafts.Few years ago a bank and a non-govt. orgn. has organized a workshop to build the capacities of stone crafts but greater efforts with funds to improve their skill, living is needed in this Mahabharatian site. Few photographs taken by the scholar of this area are given.

Biraat Sena- Mahabharatian relics

The existence of Biraat Sena in this Mahabharatian famous matsyadesa signifies that, Raja Biraat belongs to this region and interestingly a troupe called "Biraat sena" is in existence since long. They might have ascendants to the members of Biraat-sena(military) community. This sena this month staged a dharna in protest on the rising terror menace in the country and paid tribute to the deceased persons of Mumbai blast at Taj. The solidarity it expresses from far away a place from Mumbai speaks the greater consciousness of this sena. This sena is led by persons of

Mahanta community. Mahanta's are neither tribals nor general- their physical features are sharp, tallsome of their habits are similar to local tribes & some are like general higher castes. They might have descendants of Biraat Raja's army, believes many,as a number of material evidence signifies that like their lifestyles, their taste for superior quality,their demand from exclusion from ST list before independence & now for reinclusion in this same list, their livelihood pattern mostly by cultivation, cow, cattle rearing & dependence on agriculture etc.

Sanskruti Bhavan & Chaitra Parva'

The much awaited Sanskruti-Bhavan (cultural center) of the district which was under costruction since last few years was inaugurated by hon'ble Chiefminister of the state, just a day before the famous chaitra-parva. The new cultural complex, a two-storied building grandeur official complex was built at a cost of around 65 lakh it is known from cultural deptt. sources and is situated just infront of the famous chaitra-parva ground or 'chhau-padia'. The cultural complex would synthesise the various aspects of rich cultural heritages of this region and it would of great use for researchers in coming days. The Fellow also engraphed an article compiling several aspects of famous chhau dance popularly known as chaitra-parva here where this folk dance tradition is still alive since the Bhanja kings in the minds of people in this region. A description writeup on this famous dance form was made by the Fellow in contribution to this cultural dance form in a seperate published form.

Simleswara-pitha of Similipal

Simleswara pitha in this famous Similipal region is another cultural heritage site of ancient years situated by

Budhabalanga river in Golmundhakata grampanchayat under Bangiriposi block. The village Simla was surrounded with river & dense forest and legend has it that a black cow crossing the river came to this dense forest stood on a black stone without the knowledge of anyone. Once the cowherd boy Ram Behera followed this black cow and found that after crossing river Balanga it reached to a particular spot and stood there to pour milk on a black stone. The cowherd boy told this tale to his owner Fakir Giri which confirm that it is the miracle of Lord Shiva. Thereafter the simla villagers constructed a palm roof house over it and which was lateron developed into a temple by the local zamindar Minaketan Das in 1915 .The festivities of this Simleswara-pitha is spiritually uplifting under the scenic Similipal foothills.

Purnachandra Industrial Centre

This is one of the heritage building since the Bhanja kings have enriched the local region with their timeless contribution. Maharaja Purna chandra BhanjDeo the son of Sri Ramchandra Bhanj Deo was adolscent & reading at Mayo college, Ajmer at the time of the death of his father. The then British Court of wards Mr Philips & Mr Peck took the reins of Mayurbhanj state till 1920, he matures into kingship. Maharaja Purnachandra BhanjDeo was a benevolent ruler like his father and could be equal to Mughal king, Shahjehan for his lavish royalty & construction of timeless, palatial buildings which stand today as heritage site. Infact many buildings, forts of grandeur today witnessed to his contribution. Inorder to accelerate the technical progress, skill to be utilized for industrial purpose of the youths, he setup the one & only PCI popularly known as Purna Chandra Industrial Centre where students were provided free training by instructors in the areas of plumbing, stitching, knitting, embroidering. Maharani Takhatkumari undertook the entire cost for this complex which today stands as a symbol of rich cultural heritage site. Lateron after the merger of Mayurbhanj state, the state govt. took the reins of this technical training center and converted into exclusively for women in 1998. Thereafter many addition on the frontage of this heritage building like a stage-platform for cheap publicity by few has reduced its glory. Two view of this heritage structure is given.

Banabihari Mandir

Banabihari temple of Shri Krishna was dedicated by the Maharani Takhatkumari on the lake side at Takatpur. This heritage temple was remained neglected for years together till it was recovered from dilapidated condition on the initiatives of few youths which is gradually restored to its pristine glory. This dilapidated heritage temple site was covered by this Fellow on photographs, which todays under the management of debottar department.

Jhinjhir-bandh' Jubilee Park

The Bhanja kings Belgadia palace is surrounded with a natural lake popularly known as Jhinjhir-bandh meaning chain –lake which was stated to be the place of a deity. Lateron this lake was beautified with a park called Jubilee park and many a flower, fruit garden with sitting arrangements were erected to upgrade the lake into a beautiful tourist place.

According to another popular folklore, once a cowherd boy was guarding the cows and found one of its milchcow is not in the group. He made frantic search of this cow and found it in the bank of river Gangahaar where it was standing near a kakharu leaf tree and milk was pouring from its body. The next day he also found that this partcular cow is regularly going to that particular spot and sprinkling milk underneath this kakharu tree. He narrated this entire incident to villagers who came and digged the place and found Shiva linga, which later on led for establishments of today's famous Kakharua Baidyanath Pitha. A nuimber of villagers had donated each three maan (around a bigha) of land for this pitha for which this area is known as Manatri meaning three- mana and lateron Bhanja Kings were instrumental for constructing this heritage site structure.

This heritage-cultural temple was probably built during later 14th & early 15th century AD according to few other scholar- historians, when the famous Puri Gajapati Raja Kakharua Dev and in Mayurbhanj Maharaja Balabhadra BhanjDeo was ruling this region. During the visit of Puri-Gajapati the construction of this temple might have begun. Another mythology holds that during 1556 AD it was built by Mahaaja Baidyanath BhanjDeo who was also the builder of famous Shri Hari Baladev jew(Jaganath) temple in Baripada. The fact is historically verifiable as the structures, domes, natamandir of Kakharua pitha are largely identical with this Jagannath temple and it is quite different from usual shiva temples. He established the idols of Lord Jagannath in this pitha hence an ideal place of worship for Hari (Vishnu) & Hara (Shiva). Everyday the temple includes a kakharu as its prasaad and despite a shiva-pitha it usually observes all the festivals of Jagannath temple with equal fervour & grandeur like ratha-yatra, devasnan, jhulan, dolapurnima. But the most important & unique festival here is Maha Shivaratri which usually observed for a fortnight every year with lakhs of devotees thronging from allover. This rich heritage site & temple have hundreds of acres of land engaged by Bhanja rulers for the smooth management of deity & temple with grandeur. Baba Kakharua Baidyanath is surrounded with Shri Loknath, Shri Maliknath, Shri Kundanath, Shri Barahnath, Shri Swapneswarnath apart from Mahveer-Hanuman, Maa Durga.

The Fellow-scholar covers this rich cultural zone to capture the gaiety of heritageness with its raw flavour during Maha Shivaratri and the most scenic part is the appearance of deity from the river bed. A number of photo-essays with a published report in Oriya on this site is given herewith exclusively to depict the unique heritageness of this place.

Mahabharatian interaction

The number of heritage structures, monuments despite scorching heat wave and put an attempt to bring back the ancient memory of this Matsyadesa of Mahabharat fame, presently named as Mayurbhanj. The Fellow had interacted with two scholars in this regard and brought the ambience of Mahabharat fame matsyadesa which is symmetrically manifesting on observance of folklore, physical structures along with repleting memory of localities. The biggest discovery is: there is an area known as Paanch-pidh which is locally known as 'village for five' which have villages/areas in the names of Paanch-pandavas of Mahabharat fame. These are Arjuna-pidh or village-Arjuna Judhistir-pidh, Bhim-pidh etc which many believes that, perhaps habitated by the Paandavs during their agyaat - basa to this region, far away from Hastinapur. However no scholars or researchers of repute have worked upon this idea so far which is gaining strengthen with evidences of Paandavas- agyaatbasa period in this matsyadesa - Mayurbhanj.

Purnachandra Mandir

This famous heritage monuments was built by Maharani Takhatkumari , the wife of Maharaja Purnachandra Bhanj Deo whose premature death put the maharani into sorrow and she built a structure in the name of her late husband to commemorate their loving memory. This structure is known as Purnachandra Mandir, is situated amidst sprawling 3 acres of garden near the Maharaja's court office chamber which today housed district Magistrate office. This heritage building was built during 1928 and every year on 7 April, the demise day of late Maharaja was observed with pomp & ceremony by giving alms to poor & food to hungry by the descendants of Maharajas. The garden aross this structures is decorated with number of rare variety of flowers, plants, trees and is managed by the royalty till this day. Inside it, the statue of Maharaja Purachandra BhanjDeo is worshipped.

Baripada Club

This ancient heritage building was constructed by the royalty during 50's which was used by royals, british-sahebs & other important dignitaries which was later on managed by common men with changing times and presently high officials, other dignitaries used it. This heritage structure has since long providing a major cultural hub for many in this city of royalty.

Banthia-Jaganath Mandir

Apart from Shri Shri HariBaladev jew-Jaganath temple built by Maharaja Baidyaath Bhanj Deo in 1575, there is another unique temple of Lord Jaganath popularly known as San-Jaganath or Banthia-Jaganath. The idols of Jaganath, Balavadra, Suvadra are usually very small, approximately half of the length of the usual Jaganath idols. The temple was built by Maharaja Srinath Bhanj Deo during 1863-1867 AD. This ancient temple follows all the rituals of Jaganath temple and is situated in today's center of the town. Its adjacent areas have been encroached & constructed by many as a result this ancient temple have shrinked never before. The most interesting feature is: its rathyatra. A small chariot (rath) is erected which is usually pulled by children below 14 years every year. This Banthia (small) Jaganath have everything come in small sizes starting from its idol to chariot. Its mausibadi, the place where Lord Jaganath, Balavadra, Suvadra rests for nine days is being observed at nearby Sanskrit −tol -college which was also built during this period. Though a little bit restoration work of this heritage structures made some years back, the gradual encroachments from all its side and the administrative inability to remain vacant this heritage zone has gradually diminishing the historicity of this temple.

Christian Cemetry

The royalty of Mayurbhanj was kind hearted & each ruler has displayed his passion for secularism long before secularism has engraved in the Indian constitution. This has tremendously boosted the images of Bhanja Rulers. Their policy with all - be it muslims, Christians, Hindus, Sikhs or Santhal- was same; welfare of all. Even Maharajas like Sri Ramcandra BhanjDeo had patronized Christians in many ways for which a number of Christian hamlets, institutions, organizations grew up over these years. Lands, funds and royal patronage were extended to Christian minority community to grew up as a special religion. This royal patronage gave them immense morale to develop a strong Christian base here unlike any other areas in the state. Maharaja Sri Ramchandra BhanjDeo has given land for construction of churches, cemetry in 1902 by a royal-sanand (royal-order) on which a number of churches and the lone Cemetry was constructed. The Cemetry today found enroute national highway –5 and exists just at the Murgabadi circle. This cemetry have housed several Christian preachers, functionaries who came here to preach new things and is a rest house amidst serene surroundings till today. The area was earlier peaceful but today its main door is also encroached for the use of a local fish, meat bazaar. Its southern side is covered by an upcoming nursing home by few as a result the glory, the ambience it was earlier exuding have greatly diminishing with each passing day. Chances are, if this heritage site is not protected with strong measures, than soon this cemetery of a community would lost to builders, encroachers.

Nrutya-kothi of Bhanja's

The journey in this Mahabharat fame Matsyadesa with encounters to a number of issues affecting the cultural heritage institutions with the onslaught of time. The Bhanja rulers were patrons of aesthetics, art & culture. A palace- heritage building was devoted by Bhanja rulers for promotion of classical & other forms of dance. This two storied heritage building was famous in the name of nrutya-kothi or dance palace during royalty. It was learnt that a number of well known dancers from all over the country used to perform their dancing skill and highly rewarded by Bhanja rulers. Built during the time of

Maharaja Sri Ram Chandra Bhanj Deo this heritage building was remained neglected for years together and is encroached & surrounded by some illegal dhabawallas who have opened hotels in front of this heritage building .Even few timber mafias have turned this heritage palace for keeping their illegally cut timbers from local forest as no inspecting officer could ever search this heritage building premises. Lateron this palace was taken by govt. and the district food, supply department functions from this palace. But the palace has developed cracks & unsuitable for habitation and was left by officials. In 2005 this heritage palace was razed to the ground and the govt.has undertaken construction for a four storied building to put the district treasury here. Hence yesterdays nrutya-kothi is fast transforming into today's district treasury.

Karam parva – A Cultural Fiesta

The local tribes as well as mahanta, kurmi, bhumij, teli, gauda, kumbhar, khandayat communities have a cultural jamboree called karam-parva Ekadasi. After the cessation of rain months the onset of winter this celebration was being observed with pomp & gaiety. This heritage cultural trends was also observed during the Bhanja's in the Mayurbhanj palace itself, the elders say. Unmarried girls were putting black & green grams,kolatha- a local pulse grown here in a bamboo base locally known as dala'. After putting all these pulses two days before the celabration it generates sprouts on which the leaves & branches of karam tree were planted known as 'Jawa' which is being worshipped by all .During worship the songs they used to sang were in the language of malwa- used by mahanta community. In a village several household put two branches of karam leaves tree and worship it on fasting to fulfill their heartfelt desires .The karam devata is believed to be a brahmin Raja once upon a time and his symbol is keli-kadamba tree- a locally grown plant ,who had lost everything -wealth, power, position & become directionless and even used to stay in a village as a farmer. Since then to commemorate his ordeals, his subjects were believed to be observing karamparva. The typical village flavour dominates the entire karam puja day whose sentiment dates back to centuries, said a number of village elders.A published article is given by the fellow on this typical cultural fiesta.

Kurmi's Cultural demand

The kurmi-mahanta community have agitated over their inclusion again into ST fold. Their culture were of like a tribal community and long back they had demanded to declare them into general category but of late they have started realizing that re inclusion into ST fold would give them better advantage & hence agitations in the forms of meeting ,community mobilisation is found to be raising its ugly head. Some call it politics but some view it as a social malady but such a twist have given a new turn to their cultural affinity in this Mahabharatian-matsyadesa region again.

Maa Hingula-Pitha Temple

The fellow covered a number of Heritage institutions to document the glory of Mahabharatian era -Matsyadesa in this region. The road en -route to Badsahi-khunta comes a big jungle where the famous Maa Hingula temple is situated and considered a very powerful deity by many in this region. She provides all fulfillment whosoever wishes anything at her feet. Mata was 'appeared' under a peppal tree where the villagers had erected a temple. It grew into become an institution with active support of devotees making it a fund of around Rs 80 lakh. . In 2006 there was dispute over the two groups of sevayats who claims the huge fund for themselves. It led into legal battles and the local administration to interfere in the matter and last year the court gave a ruling in favour of one group who took away all the funds and even shifted the entire deity to few kilometers away from this main pitha. However few other devotees again worship her under the same tree where she appeared first and within a year there is again rush for devotees in this place. The worship is done in a very systamatic manner, first near the jajna-kunda the devotee is put on a 'sankalpa' and thereafter puja is being performed in the main temple. In a specific date of each year, Maa Hingula-yatra is performed where everything pours into a big fire pond and it was celebrated by lakhs of devotees in this region. There is also a wish-fulfilling tree behind the temple where devotees ties spade to fulfill their wishes and Maa Hingula is believed to be most powerful in fulfilling her devotees wishes and it is one of the reason that lakhs throngs to this sacred place even if it is situated deep inside the forest.

NH Inspection Bunglow

The Bhanja rulers were instrumental in building numbers of royal establishments with grandeur which withstood all the tribulations of time. This NH- IB or todays national-highway inspection bunglow was built by Maharaja Sri Ramchandra Bhanj Deo where the British sahebs like Andrew Fraser was staying to supervise the railway work before 1905. The sahebs after construction of railway here left and the same building was converted an inspection bunglow by govt. Its British era construction style and simple texture give it a look of a saheb-bunglow which still able to maintain its heritageness.

Circuit House

The Bhanja rulers were adopter of modernity, way ahead of their times and in this regard the exposure of Sri Ramchandra Bhanj Deo with western cultures, visit & interaction with Britishers all led the Maharaja to construct a lavish building during 1935-37 which is known as Circuit House or Bishram Bhavan. It is since then used as a rest house for visiting dignatories to this region like ministers, governors, high officials coming from state govt. or Centre . They used to take rest after a day long circuitory-official visits in this area. This heritage building is one of the most lavish building which has also upgraded by the successive govt's to suit to the changing needs of the time. This heritage building has enough space for keeping numbers of vehicles as well as several suites to accommodate a number of visiting dignitories to this area. In 2005 a major addition was made by district collector, V K Pandiyan when he built a mansion behind this heritage bunglow to accommodate more numbers of visiting dignitories simultaneously. This has added new dimension to this heritage bunglow.

Railways : Narrow – Broad gauge

As stated earlier the Maharaja was keen that his subjects should avail journey facilities at a lesser price and railway was best option. The historical Rupsa-Talbandh railway track in narrow-gauge is a rare historical monuments like the Darjeeling railways. In 1905 this train line was opened and linked at Rupsa which connects with major railways of the country. After the demise of Bhanja rulers this narrow-gauge train was cut short between Rupsa-Bangriposi and again between Rupsa-Baripada for a long. Many of its historic viewed tracks especially between Bangriposi to Talbandh inside the famous Similipal sanctuary was a rare feat which is no more today. Its historic tracks are also gradually disappeared and it took 100 yeas - in 2005-06 to convert this railway from narrow to broad gauge by the present govt after years of demand. Its halting station like krishnachandrapur, Betnoti, Jugal, Jugpura, Thakurtota amidst sylvan surroundings, all were built by Bhanja rulers which has now upgraded and a train between state capital Bhubaneswar - Baripada is running presently. But the historic train & its stations are still a rare monuments to watch by many visitors.

Baptist Church

The Bhanjas were secular as they allow all religion to flourish simultaneously whose evidence is popularization of Christianity. Apart from famous KCPur church both the Catholic & Protestant groups were promoted by Maharaja's and on their given land, both the sects had developed their respective churches. This Baptist church built during 1928 is situated in front of the Maharaja's Durbar – todays court office. This church was become the abode of many missionaries like Graham Staines who with their dedicated works had flourish the glory of this ancient institution. After his brutal killing in 1999, the church management has erected a hospital in memory of Staines where services to poor & leapers have taken up as a mission . Every Sunday here Christians assembled to Pray God.

Maa Santoshi Temple

In last one decade the tremendous devotion & fulfillment of wishes of several led to construct this Maa Santoshi temple which grew up from a heap of stone into glittering idols where thousands visits daily to worship her and more especially on Friday where women keep solah-sukravaar-vrata for their wish fulfillment and as a matter of focused devotion. The Maa Santoshi temple was grew up on the sole contributions of many devotees- again an established proof of peoples beliefs and faith in a higher power. Similar another temple is : Tarini temple on the road to Banthia-Jaganath temple where thousands gathered especially on Tuesday and it become an abode of power center.

Development : committed or political !

The Mahabharat fame Matsyadesa –Mayurbhanj this month again witnessed a number of violence with several bandhs for politicizing the issue of cessation of Mayurbhanj by tribal political outfits – Jharkhand Morchas. It has snowballed the agitation for reiterating its demand for taking this district along with two other- Keonjhar, Sundergarh – all forests, mineral rich to adjacent Jharkhand state for a greater Jharkhand. The intellectuals to commonmen, all have agitated and several bandhs was organized demanding boycott of jharkhandi leaders. The Fellow-scholar also came with informative published reports which opens the pandoras box. It says presently all the three tier govt.-from Panchayat to Parliament are in the control of Jharkhandi leaers since last 20 years directly and the amount of pilferage of development funds by them is unimaginable.Their tendency to grab more with blackmail politics has become the biggest hurdles for Mayurbhanj's development. The Fellow also gave a roadmap for Mayurbhanj's development by publishing a researched articles that – mere slogan is not enough,what is needed is strong commitment for development of this region. The Sal leaves- khali,dona;the Sabai grass – from rope to other items-units which are operational allover and eighty percent tribals of this region eke out their living out of it needed to be strengthened,as no organized effort was ever made by anyone,or whatever was made is inadequate. The number of closed indutrial units like Paper board unit at Dantiamuhan, the sugarcane factory at Jharpokharia, the powerloom of Takatpur and many more sick units needed to be revived. The state Bamboo Board need to invest in the huge bamboo sector,so as to tame the resing unemployment ration & growing social disturbances. The research findings were first of its kind & unique and also gave a roadmap to development of Mahabharat fame Matsyadesa –Mayurbhanj district.

Merger-Division of Mayurbhanj

This month witnessed a major spurt in violence on the cessionist demand of Jharkhand party for division of Mayurbhanj district adjacent to Jharkhand state. The demand of bifurcation of Mayurbhanj state was stiffly opposed by people allover against the jharkhandis who took the govt. to ransom for giving support during the vote of confidence held in this month. It has a greater significance with regard to the cultural identity of this region apart from its political milieu. Mayurbhanj, the old Matsyadesa where paandavas spent one year during their agayaatbasa has a rich cultural history which was in its zenith during the Bhanja Kings. In 1935-36 Mayurbhanj state was the first royalty to initiate the process of democracy with the involvement of people which led the way to its partial bifurcation at the time of merger. As areas like Sareikela, Kharswan, Chakulia, Fenko, Bankura,

Dhalbhumgarh, Olmara were bifurcated from its royal map to adjacent Bihar-Jharkhand-Bengal-Odisha areas. Since then the odia people living in these belts are undergoing with an identity conflict as they were subjected to the influence of an alien culture or a mixed one of Bengali-odia-Bihari influences simultaneously. This has created a wide gap in these Mayurbhanjities who were once subject of princely state .In 1999, the demand of Jharkhand state was curved out from Bihar and people thought the Jharkhand politics have been subsided. But the cheap way of popularity by few political leaders has put flame on the fire as they have reiterated for making a greater Jharkhand by again curving out Mayurbhanj and two other districts from Odisha. The people came out to street to oppose such divisive demands as it would create more cultural conflicts in the persons residing in this region. This even led to violent demonstration & proves that further cultural divisions in lines of cheap politics by few would endangered the region's distinct cultural identities of these people. The tribal culture amalgamated with ethnic history and a rich heritage has so far able to retain the distinct identity of societies here which would crack to ground, if further politicalised bifurcation would come to replay. It again echoed the distinct cultural identity of Mayurbhanj.

Bhanja Rulers: The Builder of Modern Mayurbhanj

The Bhanja rulers are the builders of modern Mayurbhanj, like Akbar was for the Mughals. However the North Odisha University has a prime responsibility to introduce a course curriculum on Mayurbhanj History, its ruling dynasties -the Bhanja rulers who had started their reign since 612 AD from Adi Singh to Pradeep Chandra

BhanjDeo. Their benevolent contribution has immensely contributed the social, economic & other developments in an era when many kingdoms were grappled with injustice, poverty & penury. The history of Mayurbhanj or Bhanja Rulers were not only the times & life of royalty but it would also be a parallel journey into the history of other trends,persons like socio-economic-cultural ,scholarly pursuits - art,literature and also persons like Gopal Praharaj-the author of Purnachandra odiya Bhashakosh ; Gopabandhu Dash-the doyen of Satyabadi & also the states the then vice-chairman ;Fakirmohan Senapati-the vysakabi ,Utkal gaurav Madhusudan Das,Radhanath Ray,Gobinda Chandra Mohapatra-author of translated Mahabharat,Harekrishna Mahatab-the strongman of odisha who had played a pivotal role in Mayurbhanj's history & many others who were patronized & promoted by Bhanja kings.

Art, culture, painting,s culpture, governance, judiciary, banking, railway, educational developments, livelihood generation in every sector & sphere,Mayurbhanj and its rulers played a very significant role. They were modern to the sense that, they allowed an Airplane landing zone during IInd world war, formed a Cooperative with the British cooperative father Sir Daniel Hamilton,construct Baldiha, Haldia, Badjore dams,even generated electricity from the flowing streams of Similipal sanctuary which are very modern concepts & way ahead of their times and the Bhanja Rulers with their outlook could dreamt and acted on it. For their such advancement of ideas & its implementation, they deserve specific recognition in this Mayurbhanj History course-curriculum like the Delhi & many other Universities since its beginning has implemented special couses on the history of Mughals & other Sultans, Laxmibai, Malviya as a special study package & part of their tribute to those rulers ,great minds on whose soil,contribution it stands today.

A group of Scholars need to be evolved to study their contributions in the overall development allover Odisha, India which is not only confined to Mayurbhanj alone. Starting from their funding support to Benaras Hindu University (BHU)under the invitation of Sri Madan Mohan Malviya to Utkal University where Sir Pratap Chandra BhanjDeo was the first Chancellor ;for Bhanja rulers unique contributions to the educational development allover the state to settingup of a Chair ; from Sri Ramchandra BhanjDeo Medical college to promotion of Mayurbhanj Chhau about which this generation & coming also is completely unaware and ask very often : who are Bhanja Rulers - what is their contributions ?

The NOU-North Odisha University today stands as their first contributions, as dating back to 1924 the Maharani Takat Kumari has donated around 267 acres of land for the proposed university. Does it not unobligatory on our part if this university wouldnot incorporate a special study-course-curriculum on them ? The beginning of a course on Bhanja Rulers of Mayurbhanj would also need the task for marathon research, documentation to compile the unorganized datas in this proposed department of Mayurbhanj History. It is time that the intelligent leaders of the state must put all their effort to start this new department & course as a major tribute to Bhanja kings, kingdoms before the new generation would ask – who is Pratap Chandra Bhanj !!!

MANAGEMENT OF HERITAGE ART

CULTURAL INSTITUTIONS
BHANJA- VIGNETTE IN MAHABHARAT FAME MATSYADESA - MAYURBHANJ

Bhanja's were ruler par-excellence as they believed in peoples overall development. Originally migrated from Jaipur, Rajsthan-Bhanja's laid down the dynasty of ruling in the year 598 AD onwards whose saga continues till the merger of Mayurbhanj state in January 1, 1949. A peep into the chronology of Bhanja kings ruled in Mayurbhanj state-believed to be the Mahabharat fame Matsyadesa.

Order   of
Succession
    From – To: A D

----

1.   Maharaja   Jai Singh
598 – 618
2.   Adi   Bhanj Deo
    618 – 656
3.   Nilambar   Bhanj Deo
656 – 689
4.   Laxmanagraj BhanjDeo
689 - 726
5.   Biseswara BhanjDeo
    726 – 764
6.   Bharat

BhanjDeo
764- 804

7.   Dillipeswar
BhanjDeo
804 -839

8.   Bamdev
BhanjDeo
839 – 878

9.   Basudev
BhanjDeo
878 – 916

10.   Keshari
BhanjDeo
916 – 960

11.   Narayan
BhanjDeo
960 – 996

12.   Nilakantha
BhanjDeo
996 – 1028

13.   Birkeshwari
BhanjDeo
1028 – 1064

14.   Kapileswar
Bhanjdeo
1064 – 1100

15.   Trilochan
BhanjDeo
1100-1138

16.   Dasrathi
BhanjDeo
1138 – 1164

17. BhanjDeo 1164 – 1195	SriKrishna
18. BhanjDeo 1195 – 1238	Gadadhar
19. BhanjDeo 1238 – 1264	Arneswar
20. BhanjDeo 1264 – 1279	Gopinath
21. BhanjDeo 1279 – 1301	Radhakrishna
22. BhanjDeo 1301 – 1334	Prithwinath
23. BhanjDeo 1334 – 1360	Baikunthanath
24. BhanjDeo 1360 – 1390	Bireswara
25. BhanjDeo 1390 – 1423	Ramchandra
26. BhanjDeo 1423 – 1464	Balabhadra
27. BhanjDeo	Harikrushna

1464 – 1491
28.   Nilakantha
BhanjDeo
1491 – 1520
29.   Santei
BhanjDeo
        1520 – 1556
30.   Baidyanth
BhanjDeo
   1556 – 1600
31.   Jagannath
BhanjDeo
   1600 – 1643
32.   Harihara
BhanjDeo
        1643 – 1688
33.   Sarbeswara
BhanjDeo
1688 – 1711
34.   BirBikramaditya
BhanjDeo   1711
– 1728
35.   Raghunath
BhanjDeo
1728 – 1750
36.   Chakradhar
BhanjDeo
1750 – 1761
37.   Damodar
BhanjDeo
        1761 – 1796
38.   Maharajeswari   Sumitradevi

BhanjDeo   1796 – 1810
39.   Maharajeswari   Jamunadevi
BhanjDeo   1810 – 1813
40.   Tribikram
BhanjDeo
   1813 – 1823
41.   Jadunath
BhanjDeo
   1823 – 1863
42.   Srinath
BhanjDeo
     1863 – 1868
43.   Krushna   Chandra
BhanjDeo   1868 –
1882
44.   SriRamchandra
BhanjDeo
1882 – 1912
45.   Purnachandra
BhanjDeo
1914 – 1922
46.   Pratapchandra
BhanjDeo
1923 – 1967
47.   Pradipchandra
BhanjDeo
1967 – 2005
48.   Pravinchandra
BhanjDeo
2005 –
SECTION : C

PHOTO ESSAYS
References & Bibilography

Mayurbhanj of My Times-Gobinda Chandra Mahapatra, 1896.
Mo Samayara Odisha, Dr K C Panigrahi
Matsyadesara dana-Sirish Parida
Chaitraparva journal-Mayurbhanj pratisthana
Bhanja pradip 1934-Mayurbhanj state press
Deokund diary-TOI
Charukla ra apurva samanaya, Khiching-Hemanta Kumar Dash
Karam Ekadasi-Nepal Mohanta
Sambad Uttaraodisha edition, Nov 2007
Archaeolgical mystery of Raibania-Rabindra Senapati
Sad story of a royal building-Eastern Times, J B Dash, Nov, 08
Discovery of Mahabharatian era civilization in Itagarh, Dubigarh-JB Dash, Prajatantra & Samaya saptahiki
Subterrain of Paandavas agayatabasa-Panchpidh-Sri Krushna samal, Janabani
Ancient civilization unearthed-Indian Express, JB Dash, 1997
Pandavghera-sambad uttarodisha, 24 Jan 2010
Maa Ambika of Baripada/Vokta/Institutionalisation of Mayurbhanj chhau-JB Dash, Pratisthan journal,1998
Medias in Mayurbhanj-JB Dash, 2001
Swarnayuga pravartak Maharaja Sri Ramchandra Bhanj-Dr B.Lenka

Mayurbhanj state Gazetter-Nilamani senapati, 1957

The Author expresses his sincere gratitude to those number of brochures, book, reference journals, periodicals & scholars whose insights & support have enriched this wonderful Mahabharatian era journey in Matsyadesa-Mayurbhanj.
----- Author, Fellow.

9 789356 678101